The Ultimate Black Friday Prepper's Guide

The Ultimate Black Friday Prepper's Guide

Matthew Petchinsky

1

The Ultimate Black Friday Prepper's Guide: Mastering Shopping Strategies and Savings
By: Matthew Petchinsky

Introduction

Black Friday, known globally as the pinnacle of consumer sales and retail frenzy, has evolved far beyond its original roots. What began as a uniquely American shopping event has transformed into a worldwide phenomenon marked by frenzied crowds, irresistible deals, and unprecedented economic impact. To master the art of Black Friday shopping and ensure maximum savings, understanding its history, psychological triggers, and strategic preparation is paramount. This introduction lays the groundwork for your journey into mastering Black Friday strategies with precision and confidence.

Overview of Black Friday's History and Evolution

The term "Black Friday" first appeared in the 1960s in Philadelphia, where police used it to describe the chaos that ensued on the day after Thanksgiving when hordes of suburban shoppers flooded the city, clogging streets and causing traffic headaches. It was only in the late 20th century that retailers across the U.S. embraced the day, recognizing it as an opportunity to turn a profit—literally moving from "in the red" to "in the black," hence the name.

In the early years, the deals were limited to brick-and-mortar stores, creating a culture of lining up at dawn and camping outside stores to secure coveted items. However, with the advent of technology and e-commerce, Black Friday has evolved dramatically. Today, it extends beyond a single day, often starting days or even weeks in advance with "early Black Friday" sales. The rise of Cyber Monday has also played a pivotal role, adding a digital layer that makes the shopping event accessible globally. This shift has made preparation more crucial than ever, with savvy shoppers needing to navigate both in-store and online deals to maximize their savings.

Black Friday has evolved from local shopping chaos to an international event where even countries that do not celebrate Thanksgiving have adopted the sales tradition, making it a global affair with billions of dollars exchanged in mere hours.

The Psychological Triggers of Black Friday Shopping

The allure of Black Friday is not solely in the promise of great discounts. Retailers leverage a range of psychological triggers that influence consumer behavior, making strategic shopping an essential tool for shoppers who wish to avoid falling prey to impulse buys or overspending.

Scarcity and Urgency: Retailers create a sense of urgency by using terms such as "limited time only" or "while supplies last." This scarcity principle taps into the human fear of missing out (FOMO), compelling shoppers to act quickly, often leading to hasty decisions. The psychological impact of time-bound offers can override logical thinking, prompting a rush to purchase before the opportunity slips away.

Social Proof and Competition: The sight of long lines and stories of must-have items being sold out quickly triggers a competitive spirit among shoppers. The concept of "social proof"—the idea that something is desirable because others want it—intensifies the demand for popular products. Retailers enhance this with strategic advertising and images of bustling crowds to convey that everyone is getting the best deals, adding to the urgency to participate.

The Thrill of the Hunt: For many, Black Friday shopping is a game where the thrill of finding the best deal or snagging an elusive product acts as a powerful motivator. This excitement, coupled with the anticipation of victory, stimulates dopamine production, making the shopping experience both addictive and rewarding.

Understanding these triggers helps shoppers prepare mentally and stay focused on their plans, avoiding common pitfalls that come with the rush and excitement of Black Friday shopping.

Importance of Strategic Preparation for Maximum Savings

In a landscape filled with enticing deals and marketing ploys, strategic preparation is not just beneficial—it's essential. Without a game plan, it is easy to become overwhelmed or succumb to impulse buying, which can erode potential savings and lead to post-shopping regret.

Budgeting and Financial Planning: The foundation of any effective Black Friday strategy is a well-thought-out budget. With deals on everything from electronics and appliances to clothing and travel packages, knowing how much you're willing to spend and what you're prioritizing is crucial. Establishing clear limits helps maintain financial health and ensures that you get the most value out of your shopping experience without unnecessary splurges.

Research and Tools: Armed with the right tools, shoppers can compare prices, monitor product availability, and track historical pricing to confirm if a deal is truly a bargain. Using apps and websites that alert users to price drops or exclusive discounts can be game-changers in saving both time and money.

Timing and Strategy: Planning when and where to shop allows for more strategic spending. Whether it's prioritizing in-store early morning doorbusters or timing online purchases for flash sales, having a flexible and well-researched approach maximizes savings and minimizes the stress of navigating crowded stores or high-traffic websites.

Staying Safe and Savvy: With the convenience of online shopping also comes the risk of scams and data breaches. Ensuring that cybersecurity measures are in place and recognizing reputable sites from fraudulent ones are key components of strategic preparation.

In summary, strategic preparation for Black Friday is about much more than checking off items on a list. It requires thoughtful budgeting, an understanding of marketing psychology, and leveraging technology to ensure that each purchase contributes to overall savings. This guide will walk you through every step of preparation so that you can approach Black Friday not just as a day of deals but as a finely tuned opportunity to achieve maximum value with minimal stress.

Chapter 1: Laying the Groundwork for Black Friday Success

Black Friday, with its promise of incredible deals and limited-time discounts, can be an overwhelming experience without a structured plan. The key to navigating this consumer frenzy and coming out victorious is to start with a solid foundation. Laying the groundwork for Black Friday success begins with setting clear goals, understanding the types of deals worth pursuing, and fostering a mindset of patience and focus. This chapter will guide you through these crucial first steps, ensuring that you start your Black Friday preparations on the right foot.

Setting Clear Shopping Goals

Before you step into a store or log onto your favorite e-commerce site, you need to set clear and realistic shopping goals. These goals will act as your compass, helping you navigate the myriad of sales and discounts while keeping your spending under control.

1. Define Your Priorities

Identify the main categories you plan to shop for, such as electronics, home appliances, clothing, or holiday gifts. Start by listing items that are a necessity, followed by items that would be nice to have if budget permits. This helps keep your focus on essential purchases while allowing room for a few indulgences if opportunities arise.

Example: Your must-have list might include a laptop for work, a new TV for the living room, and holiday gifts for family members. Secondary items could include smaller tech gadgets or home décor items that are discounted.

2. Set a Budget per Category

Once you have a prioritized list, allocate a budget to each category. This prevents overspending and helps distribute your finances in a balanced way. If your total budget is $1,000, you might decide to allocate $600 for electronics, $200 for clothing, and $200 for gifts. This division ensures that you're not swayed by flashy discounts that don't align with your original goals.

3. Determine Your Non-Negotiables

Some items are non-negotiable due to their necessity or the expected size of their discount. Mark these items as high-priority, ensuring they are the first ones you pursue when sales begin. Non-negotiables could be larger purchases like household appliances or work-related equipment that require both planning and immediate action when deals go live.

4. Create an Action Plan

Map out the order in which you'll shop. This includes knowing which stores you will visit first, whether online or in-person, and the best times to shop to avoid peak traffic. For online shopping, bookmark product pages and ensure your accounts on major sites are logged in and payment details are updated for a smooth checkout process.

Understanding the Best Types of Deals by Category

Not all deals are created equal, and knowing what types of products typically offer the most significant savings can help streamline your shopping strategy. Here's a breakdown of the categories that generally offer the best value on Black Friday:

1. Electronics

Electronics are the cornerstone of Black Friday deals, and for good reason. Retailers often provide significant discounts on TVs, laptops, gaming consoles, and smartphones. However, it's essential to be aware of "doorbuster" deals, which may be limited in stock or available only during specific hours. Research the best-reviewed models ahead of time and know which ones you're willing to buy if the highest-end option sells out.

2. Home Appliances

Both large and small home appliances typically see deep discounts on Black Friday. This is an excellent opportunity to upgrade your kitchen gadgets, purchase a new washer and dryer, or buy that high-tech vacuum cleaner you've been eyeing. Focus on items from reputable brands that have proven durability and good reviews.

3. Fashion and Apparel

Clothing deals can vary widely, but Black Friday often sees some of the best prices on seasonal clothing and accessories. High-end brands may offer limited-time discounts, while fast fashion retailers might run site-wide promotions. Knowing which brands or stores you want to shop at helps narrow down your focus and avoid spending on items that aren't on your priority list.

4. Holiday Gifts and Toys

If holiday shopping is part of your plan, Black Friday is one of the best times to buy gifts at a lower price. Toys, games, and popular gift items are often discounted heavily as retailers anticipate the upcoming holiday rush. Make a gift list in advance so you can take advantage of these deals without feeling rushed or disorganized.

5. Travel Deals

Less commonly known are the discounts available on travel packages and experiences. Some airlines, hotel chains, and travel agencies offer Black Friday sales with reduced rates on flights, accommodations, and vacation packages. If travel is in your future plans, Black Friday can be an opportune time to secure bookings at a fraction of their usual cost.

6. Digital Goods and Subscriptions

Black Friday isn't limited to physical products. Subscriptions to streaming services, software, and digital learning platforms often come at discounted rates. This can be an excellent time to secure annual memberships or try new services at a reduced price.

Building a Mindset of Patience and Focus

Black Friday is designed to create urgency, with its limited-time deals and countdown timers. Maintaining a calm, focused mindset is crucial to sticking to your plan and making smart purchasing decisions. Here's how to cultivate this mindset:

1. Practice Pre-Sale Patience

With the advent of "pre-Black Friday" sales and early access deals, it's easy to feel pressured into making purchases before the actual event. While some early deals can be worthwhile, practice restraint and verify that these early discounts align with historical pricing data. Use price-tracking tools to see if the "sale" is genuinely worth the early buy.

2. Set Realistic Expectations

Understand that you may not get everything on your list. Popular items can sell out quickly, and trying to chase every deal can lead to frustration. A mindset of flexibility helps manage stress and makes the shopping process more enjoyable. If a high-priority item sells out, have a backup plan or consider waiting for post-Black Friday deals, like Cyber Monday.

3. Focus on Quality over Quantity

The lure of low prices can tempt shoppers to fill their carts with items they don't need. Remind yourself that quality and long-term satisfaction with a purchase matter more than simply getting the most items for the lowest price. Evaluate potential purchases based on their usefulness, durability, and relevance to your initial goals.

4. Create a Calm Shopping Environment

Whether shopping from home or venturing out to stores, setting up a calm environment is beneficial. For online shopping, this means having a quiet space, a charged device, and all your tools ready. For in-store shopping, planning your route and allowing yourself extra time to navigate crowds can minimize stress.

5. Take Breaks and Reflect

Shopping for extended periods can lead to fatigue, which impacts decision-making. Schedule breaks to reassess your list, check your budget, and make sure you're still on track with your shopping goals. Reflection helps you refocus on what truly matters and prevents impulsive purchases driven by tiredness or excitement.

By setting clear goals, understanding which types of deals are the most advantageous, and maintaining a composed, patient approach, you'll be equipped to maximize your Black Friday shopping experience. These foundational steps will ensure that you make the most of your budget and avoid the common pitfalls that come with the chaos of Black Friday.

Chapter 2: Creating a Realistic Budget and Sticking to It

A successful Black Friday shopping experience doesn't start with choosing what stores to visit or what items to purchase; it starts with a realistic, well-thought-out budget. Creating a comprehensive budget allows you to shop confidently, knowing that you're getting the best deals without financial regret later. In this chapter, we will delve into assessing your finances, strategically allocating funds, and implementing techniques to maintain budget discipline throughout the shopping frenzy.

Assessing Your Finances Pre-Black Friday

Before diving into the world of deep discounts and doorbuster deals, it's essential to have a clear understanding of your current financial standing. This step lays the foundation for a budget that aligns with your financial goals and prevents overspending.

1. Review Your Financial Situation

Start by evaluating your current financial health. This includes checking your bank balances, reviewing recent expenditures, and ensuring that essential expenses for the month (such as rent, utilities, and bills) are accounted for. Understanding how much discretionary income you have available will give you a realistic framework for your Black Friday budget.

Action Steps:

- Log into your bank and credit card accounts to review your current balances.
- Calculate your net income for the month after deducting non-negotiable expenses.
- Determine if there are any upcoming financial commitments that need priority over shopping.

2. Identify Disposable Income

Disposable income is the portion of your income that remains after all necessary expenses are paid. This is the amount you can safely allocate toward non-essential spending, like Black Friday shopping. To find this number, subtract your regular monthly expenses (housing, groceries, transportation, etc.) from your net income. Ensure that what remains is an amount you're comfortable spending without jeopardizing your financial stability.

Example: If your monthly net income is $3,500 and your monthly expenses are $2,800, your disposable income is $700. This figure will form the basis of your maximum shopping budget.

3. Establish Emergency Fund Protection

Before you allocate your budget for shopping, verify that your emergency fund is intact. The last thing you want is to dip into funds set aside for unexpected events. Ideally, your Black Friday spending should only draw from extra savings or disposable income that won't affect your financial safety net.

Allocating Funds for Must-Haves and Potential Impulse Buys

After assessing your finances and determining how much you can spend, it's time to allocate your budget wisely. The key to a successful Black Friday budget is balancing your must-have purchases with a buffer for impulse buys that may arise.

1. Prioritize Must-Have Items

Designate a portion of your budget for items that are high on your list. These are typically big-ticket items or gifts you've planned to buy, such as electronics, appliances, or special holiday presents. Prioritizing these purchases ensures you don't spend your budget on less important items and miss out on the deals you've been anticipating.

Budget Example:

- Total budget: $700
- Must-have items allocation: $500 for a new laptop and kitchen appliance
- Remaining funds: $200 for secondary purchases or flexible spending

2. Set Aside Funds for Impulse Buys

No matter how well you plan, Black Friday can present unexpected opportunities. Set aside a specific portion of your budget for impulse buys—these could be limited-time deals, items you hadn't initially considered but that offer significant value, or gifts that you realize would be perfect during the sales event. This approach prevents you from tapping into funds meant for must-haves.

Tip: Limit your impulse buy budget to 10-15% of your total budget. This control helps manage unplanned spending while still allowing flexibility.

3. Use the Envelope System (Digitally or Physically)

The envelope system, traditionally used for cash budgeting, can be adapted digitally. Create virtual "envelopes" for different spending categories within your budget. For instance, set up digital trackers or budgeting apps to allocate portions of your budget into specific categories: "Electronics," "Clothing," "Holiday Gifts," etc. This visualization helps you keep track of spending in real-time and stick to your budget.

Tool Recommendations:

- Use budgeting apps like YNAB (You Need A Budget), Mint, or PocketGuard to create and monitor your spending categories.
- Set up a simple spreadsheet with designated columns for each budget category and track expenses as you shop.

Techniques for Maintaining Budget Discipline

Setting a budget is only part of the battle; sticking to it during the high-energy shopping event is where discipline comes into play. Here are some proven techniques to help maintain budget discipline and avoid overspending.

1. Set Up Purchase Alerts

Many banking apps and credit card services offer customizable alerts for purchases over a certain amount. These alerts can help keep your spending in check by notifying you each time you make a significant purchase. This immediate feedback allows you to reassess whether the purchase fits within your planned budget.

How to Set Alerts:

- Access your online banking portal or mobile app.
- Set notifications for transactions over a specific amount or for total spending across the day.

2. Adopt the 24-Hour Rule for Non-Urgent Purchases

When shopping online, consider adding items to your cart and waiting 24 hours before finalizing the purchase, particularly for non-essential items. This pause allows you to step back and assess whether you genuinely want or need the item, helping to reduce impulsive spending.

Exception: If a deal is marked as a limited-time offer or exclusive, ensure it aligns with your priority list before bypassing the 24-hour rule.

3. Avoid Store Credit Card Temptations

Retailers often push their store credit cards with promises of additional discounts and rewards. While this can seem tempting, store cards typically come with high-interest rates and can encourage overspending beyond your budget. If you choose to use a store card, plan to pay off the full balance immediately to avoid interest charges.

Reminder: Only use a store credit card if the rewards significantly align with your planned purchases and if you are sure of paying it off in full.

4. Track Every Purchase in Real Time

Use a simple app or note-taking tool to log each purchase as you make it. This real-time tracking helps prevent the "budget blindness" that occurs when you lose track of spending during high-intensity shopping periods.

Apps to Consider:

- Goodbudget
- Wally
- A simple shared Google Sheets or Excel file accessible on your phone

5. Shop with a Trusted Accountability Partner

Shopping with a partner, whether in-person or virtually, can help keep you on track. Choose someone who is supportive but isn't afraid to point out when you're veering off-budget. This social accountability can make sticking to your plan easier and more enjoyable.

6. Regularly Reassess Your Budget During the Day

Throughout the day, take time to pause and reassess your budget. This break allows you to see how much you've spent, how much remains, and if adjustments need to be made to your plan. Set alarms or notifications to remind you to take these check-in moments.

7. Leave Room for Unexpected Expenses

Despite all your planning, unexpected expenses may still arise. Leave a small buffer (around 5-10% of your budget) that isn't allocated to any specific category. This buffer protects you from the stress of overspending and provides flexibility if you encounter an unmissable deal.

Final Thoughts

Budgeting for Black Friday is more than just putting a number on paper; it's about understanding your finances, allocating resources wisely, and using practical techniques to maintain financial discipline during the rush of sales. With a realistic budget, strategic allocations, and budget discipline tools, you'll be well-prepared to take on Black Friday shopping with confidence and control. By the end of your shopping day, you'll not only have secured great deals but also have the satisfaction of staying true to your financial goals.

Chapter 3: The Essential Black Friday Toolkit: Must-Have Apps and Websites

Black Friday shopping isn't just about planning and budgeting—it's also about leveraging the right technology to gain a competitive edge. In today's digital age, a well-equipped Black Friday toolkit, composed of essential apps and websites, can make all the difference between snagging the best deals and missing out. This chapter will cover top-rated deal-finder apps, websites for quick price comparisons, and tools that track flash sales and limited-time offers, ensuring you have everything you need at your fingertips for a successful Black Friday.

Detailed Overview of Top-Rated Deal-Finder Apps

Navigating the sea of deals on Black Friday can be daunting, but deal-finder apps simplify this process by aggregating discounts from various retailers and notifying you of the best offers. Below are some of the most effective deal-finder apps to include in your Black Friday toolkit:

1. Honey

Honey is a popular browser extension and app that automatically searches for and applies the best available coupon codes when you shop online. It also provides price tracking for specific items and notifies you when prices drop, making it perfect for planning Black Friday purchases in advance.

Key Features:

- Automatic coupon code application at checkout
- Price history charts for selected items
- Wishlist functionality that alerts you when an item's price drops

How to Use:

- Install the Honey extension in your web browser.
- Shop as you normally would, and let Honey apply coupon codes at checkout.
- Use the price tracking feature to monitor items weeks before Black Friday.

2. Rakuten (formerly Ebates)

Rakuten is ideal for earning cashback on your Black Friday purchases. The app partners with hundreds of retailers to provide cashback on qualifying purchases, which can be a great way to maximize savings during high-spend shopping events like Black Friday.

Key Features:

- Cashback on purchases from major retailers
- Exclusive deals and bonus cashback offers during Black Friday
- Quarterly cashback payments via check or PayPal

How to Use:

- Sign up for a Rakuten account and install the browser extension or app.
- Shop at participating retailers through the app or with the extension activated to earn cashback automatically.

3. Slickdeals

Slickdeals is a community-driven app where users share and vote on the best deals. This collaborative approach ensures that only the most valuable deals rise to the top, making it easy for you to identify great discounts quickly.

Key Features:

- Real-time deal alerts set by product, brand, or category
- User-generated content with upvotes to highlight the best deals
- Integration with cashback offers and promo codes

How to Use:

- Create an account on Slickdeals and set up deal alerts for specific items.
- Check the app or website regularly to stay updated on trending deals.
- Participate in community discussions for additional insights.

4. Flipp

Flipp aggregates weekly ads and flyers from various retailers, making it a perfect tool for planning your Black Friday in-store shopping. The app allows you to search for specific items and see which stores have the best prices.

Key Features:

- Access to hundreds of local and national store flyers
- Item search functionality to find the best deals in your area
- Ability to clip and save deals for a personalized shopping list

How to Use:

- Download the Flipp app and input your location to access local store flyers.
- Search for items you plan to buy and add them to your shopping list.
- Use the app in-store to price match or verify advertised deals.

5. CamelCamelCamel

For those who frequently shop on Amazon, CamelCamelCamel is a must-have tool. This price tracking website and extension provides detailed price history charts and alerts you when the price of an item drops to your desired level.

Key Features:

- Price tracking and history charts for millions of Amazon products
- Customizable price drop alerts
- Insight into whether a current deal is truly a discount or just hype

How to Use:

- Use the website or install the browser extension.
- Add items to your price watch list and set target prices for notifications.
- Check price history charts to evaluate if a current discount is the lowest ever.

Navigating Websites for Quick Price Comparisons

Quick price comparison tools are essential for making informed purchases. They allow you to see real-time prices from multiple retailers, ensuring you get the best value on Black Friday. Here are some must-use price comparison websites:

1. Google Shopping

Google Shopping aggregates prices from a variety of retailers, displaying them in an easy-to-read format. It's a powerful tool for price comparison across many product categories.

Key Features:

- Comprehensive list of prices from different retailers
- Ability to filter by price, brand, and condition (new or used)
- Links directly to the retailer's product page for seamless shopping

How to Use:

- Search for the item you're interested in on Google Shopping.
- Compare prices from different stores to find the best deal.
- Use filters to narrow down your options by price range and other criteria.

2. PriceGrabber

PriceGrabber allows you to compare prices from thousands of retailers, providing a straightforward interface that lets you quickly assess the best deals on items from electronics to clothing.

Key Features:

- Wide range of categories and retailers
- Integrated coupons and deals for added savings
- Direct links to purchase items from your chosen retailer

How to Use:

- Enter the product name or keyword in the search bar on the PriceGrabber site.
- Sort results by price, retailer, or other preferences.
- Click through to the retailer's site to complete your purchase.

3. ShopSavvy

ShopSavvy is a mobile app that lets you scan barcodes while shopping in-store to compare prices online. This feature is especially useful when you're shopping in person and want to verify that you're getting the best deal.

Key Features:

- Barcode scanning for on-the-spot price comparisons
- Alerts for price drops on saved items
- Integration with both online and local store prices

How to Use:

- Download the ShopSavvy app and scan an item's barcode.
- Review the price comparisons from various retailers.
- Save items to receive notifications when prices drop.

Tools to Track Flash Sales and Limited-Time Offers

Flash sales and limited-time offers are the highlights of Black Friday, but they can be easy to miss without the right tracking tools. Here are some apps and tools that can help you stay on top of these time-sensitive deals:

1. DealNews

DealNews aggregates limited-time offers and flash sales from major retailers, making it easy to keep track of short-lived discounts. The site updates frequently, ensuring you always have the latest information.

Key Features:

- Daily updates on limited-time offers
- Alerts for specific items or categories
- Verified deals to avoid misleading promotions

How to Use:

- Visit the DealNews website or download the app.
- Set up alerts for specific products or categories you're interested in.
- Check the site regularly for new and verified deals.

2. KEEPA

Keepa is another tool tailored for Amazon shoppers. It tracks price changes and highlights flash sales, ensuring you're aware of when prices drop temporarily.

Key Features:

- Real-time price tracking for Amazon products
- Notifications for flash sales and discounts
- Detailed price history charts

How to Use:

- Install the Keepa browser extension.
- Search for items on Amazon and view price history and current promotions.
- Set price drop alerts to receive notifications.

3. Slickdeals Flash Sale Tracker

The Slickdeals app includes a flash sale tracker that highlights limited-time offers shared by its community. The real-time nature of this app ensures you don't miss out on major discounts.

Key Features:

- User-generated alerts for flash sales
- Filters to narrow down sales by category or store
- Direct links to sales pages for quick access

How to Use:

- Enable notifications for flash sales within the Slickdeals app.
- Set up deal alerts for specific items or categories.
- Act quickly when alerts arrive to make the most of short-lived deals.

4. Retailer Apps

Many major retailers have their own apps that notify users of exclusive app-only flash sales. Downloading the apps of stores you plan to shop at can give you early access to these limited-time promotions.

Examples of Retailer Apps:

- Target
- Best Buy
- Macy's
- Walmart

How to Use:

- Download the app of each retailer where you plan to shop.
- Enable push notifications to receive alerts for flash sales and special offers.
- Sign in to your account and save items to your wishlist for quick access.

Final Thoughts

Equipping yourself with the right apps and websites is essential for a successful Black Friday shopping experience. Whether you're shopping online or in-store, these tools can help you find the best prices, compare deals in real-time, and stay updated on flash sales. By integrating these resources into your strategy, you'll be better prepared to navigate the frenzy of Black Friday and make confident, budget-friendly purchases.

Chapter 4: Prepping Your Tech for Maximum Shopping Efficiency

Black Friday shopping is a race against time, where every second counts. With the majority of deals now happening online, ensuring your technology is optimized for speed, security, and reliability can mean the difference between snagging that must-have deal or watching it slip away. In this chapter, we will explore how to prepare your devices for peak performance, use multiple devices and browser extensions effectively, and avoid common tech pitfalls during high-traffic shopping hours.

Device Optimization Tips for Speed and Security

Optimizing your devices before Black Friday ensures that you're not hindered by slow load times or security vulnerabilities. Here's how to prep your tech for seamless shopping:

1. Free Up Storage Space

Devices that are low on storage can experience sluggish performance, impacting how fast pages load or apps respond. Clear unnecessary files, old downloads, and unused apps to create space for your browser and shopping apps to function at top speed.

How to Clear Storage:

- **On Desktop/Laptop**: Use built-in disk cleanup tools (e.g., Disk Cleanup on Windows or Finder's Manage Storage on macOS) to delete temporary files.
- **On Mobile Devices**: Navigate to your settings and manually clear app caches and delete large, unused apps.

2. Update Software and Apps

Ensure your device's operating system, web browser, and all relevant shopping apps are updated to their latest versions. Updates often include performance enhancements and security patches, both of which are crucial for a smooth shopping experience.

Tips:

- **Browsers**: Use browsers like Google Chrome, Firefox, or Safari that support extensions and have robust security features.
- **Apps**: Ensure your shopping apps (e.g., Amazon, Target, Walmart) are updated to access the latest deals and notifications.

3. Enable Two-Factor Authentication (2FA)

Security should never be overlooked, especially when shopping online during high-traffic sales events. Enable 2FA on your accounts for an added layer of protection. This prevents unauthorized access even if your password is compromised.

Steps to Enable 2FA:

- Log into your online account (e.g., Amazon, PayPal).
- Go to security settings and enable 2FA.
- Follow the prompts to link your account with an authentication app or phone number.

4. Optimize Your Internet Connection

A fast and stable internet connection is vital during peak shopping times. Use a wired Ethernet connection for desktops if possible, as it generally provides faster and more reliable speeds than Wi-Fi. For mobile shopping, ensure you're on a strong Wi-Fi network or have a reliable mobile data plan.

Tips for Optimization:

- **Router Placement**: Place your router in an open, central location to maximize signal strength.
- **Reboot Router**: Restart your router the day before Black Friday to refresh its connection.
- **Use a VPN**: While optional, a VPN can protect your data from being intercepted, especially if shopping from public Wi-Fi. Choose a reputable, fast VPN to avoid slowing down your connection.

5. Clean Up Your Browser

Too many extensions or open tabs can slow down your browsing speed. Remove unnecessary browser extensions and close tabs to enhance performance.

Steps:

- Go to your browser's settings or extensions manager.
- Disable or remove extensions that you don't need.
- Bookmark important pages so you can close tabs without losing track of deals.

Using Multiple Devices and Browser Extensions for Fast Access

To increase your chances of securing popular items, using multiple devices and browser extensions can streamline your shopping process and give you a competitive edge.

1. Prepare Multiple Devices for Simultaneous Use

Having a desktop or laptop, tablet, and smartphone ready for simultaneous use allows you to monitor different sites and deals at once. Each device can be dedicated to a specific retailer or task, such as checking out, monitoring flash sales, or comparing prices.

Setup Tips:

- **Device Allocation**: Assign your laptop to major online retailers, your smartphone to store-specific apps, and your tablet for browsing deal aggregators like Slickdeals or Flipp.
- **Sync Accounts**: Ensure all devices are logged into the same shopping accounts with saved payment information for a smooth checkout.

2. Leverage Browser Extensions for Speed and Convenience

Browser extensions can automate time-consuming tasks like applying coupon codes, tracking price drops, and autofilling checkout forms. Here are some must-have extensions:

Popular Browser Extensions:

- **Honey**: Automatically finds and applies coupon codes at checkout.
- **Rakuten**: Alerts you to cashback opportunities as you shop.
- **Keepa**: Provides detailed price history for Amazon items and alerts for price drops.
- **LastPass**: Saves and autofills passwords and payment details for quicker checkout.

How to Use Extensions Effectively:

- Install the extensions a week before Black Friday to familiarize yourself with their functionalities.
- Customize alert settings so you're only notified about relevant deals.
- Keep extensions updated to prevent compatibility issues.

3. Streamline Payment Processes with Digital Wallets

Set up and test digital wallets like PayPal, Apple Pay, or Google Pay. These wallets offer fast, one-click payment options that can shave precious seconds off your checkout time, making it easier to secure limited-stock items.

Benefits of Digital Wallets:

- Faster checkout process with stored payment details.
- Enhanced security with encrypted transactions.
- Ability to bypass entering credit card details for every purchase.

Avoiding Common Tech Pitfalls During High-Traffic Shopping Hours

Even with the best preparation, certain tech pitfalls can slow you down or disrupt your shopping experience. Here's how to avoid them:

1. Plan for Site Crashes

It's not uncommon for high-traffic websites to crash or become unresponsive during peak shopping times. To avoid losing valuable time, have backup strategies:

Backup Strategies:

- **Open Multiple Tabs**: Load product pages in different tabs so you can quickly switch if one tab crashes.
- **Use Alternative Retailers**: Identify secondary sites or retailers that may offer similar deals.
- **Save Wishlist Links**: Bookmark items so you can reload them quickly if the site refreshes or crashes.

2. Be Wary of Phishing Sites

Cybercriminals often take advantage of major sales events by creating fake sites that mimic legitimate retailers. Always verify the URL and ensure you're on the correct site before entering any payment information.

How to Spot Phishing Sites:

- Check for "https" in the URL for secure sites.
- Avoid sites with odd spellings or subtle typos in the domain.
- Look for security certificates or badges indicating verified authenticity.

3. Prevent Slowdowns from Background Apps

Background apps and automatic updates can slow down your device during critical shopping times. Close unnecessary programs and pause software updates to free up resources.

Tips for Speeding Up Your Device:

- **Task Manager (Windows)**: Use Ctrl+Shift+Esc to open Task Manager and end non-essential processes.
- **Activity Monitor (Mac)**: Access via Applications > Utilities to identify and quit resource-heavy apps.
- **Disable Background App Refresh (Mobile Devices)**: Navigate to your settings to prevent non-essential apps from refreshing in the background.

4. Watch Out for Data Caps and Throttling

Internet service providers may throttle bandwidth during high-traffic times. To avoid this, monitor your data usage and consider upgrading to a higher-speed plan if you anticipate significant shopping activity.

Pro Tips:

- **Check Data Plans**: Ensure your mobile plan has enough high-speed data.
- **Monitor Bandwidth**: Use apps or built-in router features to track bandwidth usage during shopping.

Final Thoughts

Prepping your tech for Black Friday shopping can greatly improve your speed, security, and overall efficiency. By following these detailed device optimization tips, using multiple devices and browser extensions strategically, and avoiding common pitfalls, you'll set yourself up for a smooth, hassle-free shopping experience. With these measures in place, you can confidently dive into the sales event, ready to seize the best deals without technical difficulties standing in your way.

Chapter 5: The Art of the Shopping List

The heart of any successful Black Friday shopping strategy is a well-structured shopping list. A clear and organized list helps streamline decision-making, reduce stress, and ensure that you secure your most important items before they sell out. In this chapter, we will explore how to structure your shopping list by priority and urgency, categorize purchases for quick decision-making, and effectively use digital note apps for collaborative shopping.

Structuring Lists by Priority and Urgency

A generic shopping list is helpful, but structuring it by priority and urgency elevates its effectiveness, enabling you to focus on securing the most critical items first. Here's how to structure your list for maximum impact:

1. Divide Your List into Priority Levels

Organize your list into three main categories: High Priority, Medium Priority, and Low Priority. This approach helps you navigate your shopping day with clear direction, ensuring that the most important items are acquired first.

High Priority: These are essential items that you cannot afford to miss, such as big-ticket electronics, major appliances, or items with historically deep Black Friday discounts.

Medium Priority: These are items you want but are willing to skip if they become unavailable, such as clothing, small home gadgets, or non-essential gifts.

Low Priority: These items are non-essential and can be purchased if budget and time allow, such as novelty items, accessories, or bonus gift items.

Example:

- **High Priority**: 4K Smart TV, gaming laptop, new smartphone
- **Medium Priority**: Designer winter coat, kitchen blender

- **Low Priority**: Decorative home items, board games

2. Rank by Urgency

Within each priority category, rank items by urgency. This step refines your list even further, allowing you to identify which high-priority items should be targeted first due to limited availability or significant savings.

Urgency Indicators:

- **Time-Sensitive Sales**: Mark items that are part of a flash sale or a limited-time offer.
- **Stock Concerns**: Highlight items that are likely to sell out quickly, such as popular electronics or toys.
- **Gift Needs**: Note items that need to be purchased early for specific events or holiday gifting.

3. Note Store and Time Details

Add information to each item about which store or website you plan to purchase from and the optimal time to buy. This planning helps you map out your day, whether you're shopping online or visiting physical stores.

Example:

- **4K Smart TV** – High Priority, Urgent; Available at Best Buy at 6 AM
- **Designer Winter Coat** – Medium Priority, Flexible; Online at Macy's, anytime before 2 PM

Categorizing Purchases for Quick Decision-Making

Categorizing your list into broad and specific sections allows for quicker decision-making and smoother shopping experiences. Here's how to categorize effectively:

1. Create Broad Categories for Overall Organization

Start by dividing your shopping list into general categories, such as Electronics, Home Appliances, Clothing, Gifts, and Miscellaneous. This initial division provides a snapshot of where your focus will be, helping you allocate time and budget more effectively.

Example Categories:

- **Electronics**: TV, smartphone, gaming laptop, headphones
- **Home Appliances**: Coffee maker, air fryer, robotic vacuum
- **Clothing**: Winter coat, boots, scarves
- **Gifts**: Toys, board games, gift cards
- **Miscellaneous**: Home décor, fitness equipment

2. Subcategorize for Specific Items

Within each broad category, create subcategories that detail specific items you are targeting. This step ensures you can quickly identify the exact products you need and make faster purchase decisions.

Example:

- **Electronics**
    - 4K Smart TV (specific brand/model)
    - Smartphone (iPhone 15 or equivalent)
    - Gaming laptop (model details)
- **Home Appliances**

- Robotic vacuum (brand options)
- Air fryer (size details)

3. List Alternative Options

Include backup options for high-demand items. This flexibility is critical when primary choices sell out, allowing you to pivot quickly and still secure a similar product without extensive browsing or research.

Example:

- **Primary**: iPhone 15
- **Backup**: Samsung Galaxy S23
- **Alternative TV Models**: Samsung 4K, LG OLED if main choice is unavailable

Utilizing Digital Note Apps for Collaborative Shopping

Digital note apps are powerful tools for organizing your shopping list, collaborating with friends or family, and maintaining real-time updates as the shopping day unfolds. Here's how to use them effectively:

1. Choose the Right Note App

Select a digital note app that suits your needs, such as Evernote, Google Keep, Microsoft OneNote, or shared document platforms like Google Docs. Look for features that allow for checklists, attachments, and real-time collaboration.

Top Digital Note Apps:

- **Evernote**: Ideal for creating detailed lists, attaching web links, and sharing with others.
- **Google Keep**: Simple interface with real-time updates and collaborative features.
- **Microsoft OneNote**: Comprehensive note-taking tool with the ability to organize lists by tabs and share them easily.
- **Google Docs**: Great for creating collaborative lists that allow for edits by multiple users in real time.

2. Create and Share Collaborative Lists

For those shopping with friends or family, a shared digital list ensures everyone is aware of the game plan. Assign specific items to individuals, so team members know who is responsible for which purchase.

Steps for Collaboration:

- Create a list with checkboxes for each item.
- Label items with the assigned shopper's name or initials.
- Share the document or note link with permissions set to allow edits by the team.

Example:

- **Electronics**
    - ◦ 4K Smart TV (Alex)
    - ◦ Gaming laptop (Mia)
- **Gifts**
    - ◦ Toy set for nephew (Liam)

3. Integrate Web Links and Price Comparisons

Include direct web links to product pages and notes on price comparisons in your digital list. This feature allows for quick access to specific items and ensures you don't waste time searching for deals you previously identified.

How to Integrate Links:

- Copy the URL of the product page and paste it into your note under the item description.
- Add a brief note indicating the best price found and any promo codes applicable.

4. Update Lists in Real-Time

Keep your digital note app open during the shopping event to check off items as you secure them and note any changes or adjustments. If collaborating, team members will see updates immediately, reducing the risk of duplicate purchases or missed items.

Real-Time Benefits:

- Immediate updates on item status, such as "purchased" or "sold out."
- Alerts to teammates about shifting focus to backup options.
- Coordination on shared gift purchases to avoid confusion.

5. Use App-Specific Features for Efficiency

Explore app-specific features such as tagging, color-coding, and reminders to enhance the usability of your shopping list.

App Features:

- **Google Keep**: Use labels and color-coding to prioritize items visually.
- **Evernote**: Set reminders for time-sensitive purchases.
- **OneNote**: Use tabs to create separate lists for online vs. in-store shopping or by retailer.

Final Thoughts

A well-structured shopping list is a cornerstone of Black Friday success. By prioritizing items by urgency, categorizing purchases, and utilizing collaborative digital tools, you can stay organized, focused, and adaptable throughout the day. This proactive approach ensures that your shopping experience is efficient and that you make the most of every deal, whether you're securing must-have electronics or thoughtful holiday gifts.

Chapter 6: Timing is Everything: Planning When to Shop

In the world of Black Friday shopping, timing is crucial. Knowing when to shop can mean the difference between securing an amazing deal or missing out altogether. This chapter will guide you through understanding peak deal times, planning an hour-by-hour strategy, and coordinating with time zone differences for online exclusives to optimize your Black Friday experience.

Understanding Peak Deal Times vs. Lesser-Known Discounts

Timing your shopping right involves recognizing when peak deals are released and when lesser-known discounts might appear. Retailers often have specific times when they roll out major promotions, but understanding when to look for smaller, niche deals can also enhance your shopping strategy.

1. Identifying Peak Shopping Hours

Peak deal times are typically when retailers release their most popular discounts. These are the periods with the highest shopper traffic, both online and in-store. Familiarizing yourself with these peak hours helps you plan your day for maximum efficiency.

Typical Peak Hours:

- **Early Morning**: Many stores open as early as 5 AM or 6 AM, and major deals are often released online at midnight or in the early morning hours.
- **Midday Surges**: Around 12 PM to 2 PM, stores often replenish stock or release new waves of deals to draw in the lunch-hour crowd.
- **Evening Updates**: Some retailers introduce new deals or refresh existing ones in the late evening, typically around 6 PM to 8 PM.

2. Spotting Lesser-Known Discounts

While peak hours attract the most attention, lesser-known deals can appear during off-peak times. These discounts are typically more niche but can offer great value for those who know where and when to look.

When to Find Them:

- **Late Night or Early Morning Hours (1 AM to 4 AM)**: Some online retailers may release flash sales or exclusive discounts at off-hours to cater to night owls or international customers.
- **Mid-Afternoon Lulls (2 PM to 5 PM)**: During quieter shopping periods, you may find unscheduled markdowns or flash sales aimed at driving traffic during the lull.
- **Post-Peak Adjustments**: After the initial rush, some retailers update their pricing based on competitor activity. These adjustments can yield surprising deals if you're monitoring prices closely.

3. Tracking Trends from Previous Years

Studying past Black Friday trends can help you anticipate when major deals are most likely to appear. Look at reports or articles summarizing the timing of past Black Fridays to build a timeline of when the best deals might drop.

Mapping Out an Hour-by-Hour Strategy

An hour-by-hour strategy is essential for maintaining focus and ensuring you hit all key deals during Black Friday. This plan divides your day into manageable chunks, guiding you on when to prioritize certain types of purchases and when to take breaks for reassessment.

1. Pre-Midnight Prep (10 PM – 12 AM on Thanksgiving)

- **Finalize Your Setup**: Ensure all devices are charged, apps are updated, and browser extensions are active.
- **Log Into Your Accounts**: Log into your main shopping accounts (e.g., Amazon, Walmart, Target) with payment information saved.
- **Set Alerts**: Ensure you have notifications turned on for deal alerts from key apps and websites.

2. Midnight to 3 AM: Early Online Deals

- **Target Major Retailers**: Focus on high-priority items from big-box stores like Amazon, Best Buy, and Walmart, as they often release their biggest deals at midnight.
- **Act Fast**: Be prepared to check out quickly, as high-demand items may sell out within minutes.
- **Monitor Flash Sales**: Keep an eye on websites that announce flash sales on the hour or half-hour.

3. 3 AM to 6 AM: Niche and International Deals

- **Explore Specialty Retailers**: Look at less mainstream sites or niche retailers for specific items, like tech accessories or specialty apparel.

- **Tap into International Stores**: If shopping internationally, co-ordinate purchases according to the time zone differences to align with their sales periods.

4. 6 AM to 9 AM: Early Bird In-Store Deals

- **Visit Brick-and-Mortar Stores**: For those venturing out, early morning is the best time to grab in-store deals that aren't available online.
- **Split Responsibilities**: If shopping with others, divide stores or categories so each person tackles a different set of deals.
- **Keep Mobile Alerts On**: Stay updated on new online deals while waiting in line or shopping in-store.

5. 9 AM to 12 PM: Morning Online Refreshes

- **Second Wave of Deals**: Many retailers will release a second batch of deals in the morning to attract a new wave of shoppers.
- **Cross-Check Prices**: Use price comparison tools and apps to ensure that early morning purchases were the best deals.
- **Adjust Your Plan**: If certain items have sold out, move to backup options or adjust your budget allocation.

6. 12 PM to 3 PM: Midday Reassess and Pivot

- **Review Your Progress**: Check off completed purchases and re-assess your remaining items.
- **Take Advantage of Midday Updates**: Some retailers will refresh or extend their sales at midday.
- **Stay Hydrated and Rested**: A quick break helps maintain energy and focus for the rest of the shopping day.

7. 3 PM to 6 PM: Niche and Lower-Traffic Shopping

- **Target Niche Items**: Use this time to secure less-popular items that may have lower competition.
- **Leverage Social Media**: Monitor store accounts and deal-sharing communities for unexpected deals or announcements.

8. 6 PM to 9 PM: Evening Rush

- **Watch for New Evening Deals**: Some stores may offer "evening-only" discounts or refresh stock for a last-minute rush.
- **Review Wishlist Items**: Check if prices on wishlist items have dropped since earlier in the day.
- **Prepare for Cyber Monday**: Set alerts and save items for Cyber Monday if you didn't secure them during Black Friday.

Coordinating with Time Zone Differences for Online Exclusives

Black Friday has expanded into a global event, with retailers worldwide participating. Knowing how to coordinate with time zone differences can help you access deals that might not be available locally or appear at different times.

1. Use World Clock Tools

Ensure you're tracking relevant time zones with a world clock app or built-in clock tools on your smartphone or computer. This helps you know when deals go live on international websites.

Example Time Zones to Monitor:

- **Eastern Time (ET)**: Common for U.S. East Coast deals.
- **Pacific Time (PT)**: Used by major retailers headquartered on the West Coast, like Amazon and Costco.
- **GMT (Greenwich Mean Time)**: Useful for tracking European-based retailers.

2. Schedule Purchase Times for International Retailers

If you're shopping from stores based in different countries, make a schedule that includes their local sale times. Factor in the time difference to avoid missing a deal simply because it launched at an odd hour in your local time.

Tips:

- Use a scheduling tool like Google Calendar to set reminders and alarms for key sale start times in various time zones.
- Plan your most important international purchases first, especially if you anticipate high competition.

3. Plan for Delayed Shipping and Fees

International deals might come with shipping delays or fees that impact the overall savings. Review these potential costs before purchasing to ensure the deal remains worthwhile.

Important Considerations:

- **Customs Fees**: Check if the total cost will include additional taxes or customs fees.
- **Shipping Time**: Verify estimated delivery times to avoid waiting longer than anticipated, especially for gifts or urgent items.

Final Thoughts

Mastering the timing of your Black Friday shopping can maximize your savings and help you secure hard-to-get items. By understanding peak deal times, planning an hour-by-hour shopping strategy, and coordinating purchases across time zones, you can shop confidently and efficiently. This strategic approach ensures that you not only get the best deals but also make the most of your time and budget.

Chapter 7: Insider Tips for In-Store and Online Shopping

Black Friday can be a chaotic mix of long lines, limited stock, and intense competition, whether you're shopping in-store or online. To make the most of your shopping experience, it's essential to have a set of insider tips to navigate these challenges efficiently. In this chapter, we'll explore expert strategies for moving through crowded stores, securing your online cart before checkout rushes, and spotting and avoiding misleading doorbuster deals.

Navigating Crowded Stores Efficiently

Shopping in-store on Black Friday can be overwhelming, with aisles packed and tensions running high. However, with the right tactics, you can move through stores efficiently and grab the items you need without undue stress.

1. Plan Your Route Ahead of Time

Before heading out, map out your shopping route. Identify which stores you'll visit first and the order in which you'll visit them based on the priority of items and store opening times. This prevents backtracking and ensures you hit high-priority stores during their prime deal periods.

Tips for Route Planning:

- **Mall Layouts**: If shopping in a mall, obtain a map or familiarize yourself with the layout in advance.
- **Store Blueprints**: For major retailers, check online for store-specific maps that show where key items like electronics and appliances are located.
- **Park Strategically**: Park near exits that will allow for a quick getaway after your shopping is done.

2. Arrive Early, but Be Prepared

Getting to stores early is a tried-and-true method for securing door-busters and high-demand items, but being prepared makes all the difference.

What to Bring:

- **Shopping List**: Have your list of high-priority items and store locations printed or accessible on your phone.
- **Comfortable Clothing and Shoes**: You'll be standing and walking a lot, so wear comfortable, supportive footwear and dress in layers that can be easily adjusted.
- **Reusable Bags**: Bring your own bags to save time at checkout and navigate the store more easily.

3. Use a "Divide and Conquer" Strategy

If you're shopping with friends or family, split up to cover more ground. Assign each person a specific section of the store or list of items. This strategy increases your chances of securing multiple sought-after products simultaneously.

Pro Tip: Maintain communication through text or walkie-talkie apps to coordinate updates on item availability and checkout times.

4. Navigate Crowds with Precision

Moving through a packed store requires skill and patience. Avoid the most crowded aisles by entering through less busy sections and working your way to the center. Be polite but assertive when moving, and keep an eye out for restocking employees who may have additional items.

Techniques:

- **Stay to the Right**: Just like driving, stay to the right side of aisles to keep foot traffic flowing.
- **Avoid Choke Points**: Steer clear of displays or bottlenecks where crowds tend to gather.

- **Keep Your Items Safe**: Use your cart or basket strategically to shield the items you've already picked up from accidental (or intentional) grabs by other shoppers.

5. Prioritize Checkout Efficiency

Choose checkout lines carefully. Express lanes and self-checkout areas often move faster than regular lines. If you see an associate opening a new lane, be ready to move quickly.

Tips for Faster Checkout:

- **Mobile Payment**: If the store allows, use mobile payment apps like Apple Pay or Google Pay for quicker transactions.
- **Be Ready**: Have your payment method and any coupons or promo codes out and ready before you reach the register.

Strategies for Securing Online Carts Before Checkout Rushes

Online shopping on Black Friday is a game of speed, where items can vanish from your cart in seconds. Implement these strategies to secure your purchases before checkout rushes overwhelm the system.

1. Create Accounts and Save Information Ahead of Time

Set up accounts with your preferred retailers before Black Friday, and ensure your payment and shipping details are saved. This reduces checkout time and decreases the chances of items being snatched out of your cart while you're entering information.

Preparation Checklist:

- **Create Accounts**: Ensure you have active accounts on the sites you plan to shop from.
- **Save Payment Methods**: Enter and save payment details in advance.
- **Update Addresses**: Double-check that your shipping information is current.

2. Use "Add to Cart" Extensions

Certain browser extensions can help you add items to your cart faster by skipping extra clicks. Research and install these tools in advance, ensuring they're compatible with your preferred sites.

Examples:

- **Checkify**: Simplifies the "add to cart" process.
- **Honey**: While primarily a coupon tool, it can help streamline checkout with saved payment details.

3. Pre-Load Carts When Possible

Some retailers allow you to add items to your cart before Black Friday sales go live. Pre-load your cart with items you plan to purchase and re-fresh the page as the sale begins. Be ready to update prices if discounts don't automatically apply.

Pro Tip: Open multiple tabs for different items to speed up switching between product pages and the checkout process.

4. Use Multiple Devices and Browsers

If you're shopping for high-demand items, having multiple devices (e.g., a phone, tablet, and laptop) can increase your chances of a successful checkout. Use different browsers or incognito windows to bypass any potential session limitations from one device.

Device Strategy:

- **Main Device**: Use your fastest, most reliable device for primary purchases.
- **Secondary Device**: Keep a backup device ready in case your main device freezes or crashes.
- **Tablet/Phone**: Use mobile apps that may have quicker access or exclusive app-only deals.

5. Refresh Cautiously

Refreshing a webpage during high-traffic shopping can be a double-edged sword. While it's necessary for updates, over-refreshing can lead to site bans or freezing.

Best Practice:

- **Set a Timer**: Refresh at intervals of 30-60 seconds if the site isn't loading.
- **Avoid Over-Clicking**: Let pages load without repeated clicks that could flag your session as suspicious.

6. Complete Checkout Fast

Once you've added items to your cart, move swiftly to checkout. Use one-click payment options if available, such as PayPal, Apple Pay, or Google Pay, to minimize typing time.

Key Tip: Don't browse for additional items during checkout; secure your initial purchases first and return to shop more later if needed.

How to Spot and Avoid Doorbuster Decoys

Doorbuster deals are marketed as unbeatable prices meant to draw shoppers in, but not all are what they seem. Here's how to distinguish the genuine bargains from misleading decoys.

1. Research in Advance

Retailers often use high-profile deals to lure customers, but these deals may not always be the best available. Research the products featured in doorbuster promotions to determine their true value and quality.

Steps for Research:

- **Check Reviews**: Search for product reviews to verify quality.
- **Compare Prices**: Use price comparison tools to see if the "doorbuster" price is genuinely lower than recent averages.
- **Identify Product Versions**: Verify whether the item is a lesser-known model or an older version that's being offloaded.

2. Look for "Limited Stock" Indicators

If an advertisement says "limited quantities available" or "while supplies last," be prepared for a small number of units that will sell out quickly. These items can still be worthwhile, but only if you plan to shop as soon as doors open or the sale goes live online.

Decoding Labels:

- **"Special Buy" or "Black Friday Edition"**: Sometimes these terms are used for models specifically made for sales events, which may not have the same quality as regular items.

3. Evaluate Substitute Products

Many stores have substitute products that are not advertised as prominently but offer comparable features and better availability. Being aware of these alternatives can save you from wasting time chasing a sold-out doorbuster.

Example:

- If the latest 4K TV advertised as a doorbuster sells out, a similar model with a slightly different feature set may be available at a comparable discount.

4. Don't Fall for Bundled "Bargains"

Bundled products can sometimes seem like great deals but may include unnecessary extras that inflate the perceived value. Check if the items in the bundle are actually needed or if purchasing items separately would be more cost-effective.

Tips for Bundles:

- **Break Down the Price**: Evaluate the price of each item in the bundle to determine its individual value.
- **Check for Essential Components**: Ensure the bundle includes only items you planned to buy and won't inflate your budget unnecessarily.

Final Thoughts

Black Friday shopping requires more than just preparation; it demands strategic thinking and adaptability. By learning how to navigate crowded stores efficiently, securing your online carts swiftly, and recognizing doorbuster decoys, you'll be better equipped to capitalize on genuine deals and avoid pitfalls. Whether shopping in-store or online, these insider tips will give you the edge needed to make your Black Friday experience both successful and satisfying.

Chapter 8: Advanced Price Comparison Techniques

To maximize your savings on Black Friday, mastering the art of price comparison is essential. While basic techniques can help you find good deals, advanced strategies will enable you to confidently distinguish between genuine bargains and marketing ploys. This chapter will cover using barcode scanners and price comparison sites effectively, identifying fake discounts and inflated "regular" prices, and leveraging price match guarantees for the best possible savings.

Using Barcode Scanners and Price Comparison Sites

Barcode scanners and price comparison sites are indispensable tools for real-time price checks and decision-making. These tools empower you to instantly compare prices across multiple retailers, ensuring that you make informed purchasing decisions.

1. Barcode Scanning Apps

Barcode scanning apps are particularly useful for in-store shopping. They allow you to scan the product's barcode and instantly see its price at various online and local retailers. This helps you avoid impulse purchases and make sure you're truly getting the best deal available.

Top Barcode Scanning Apps:

- **ShopSavvy**: One of the most popular barcode scanning apps that provides price comparisons from major online and local retailers. It also offers reviews and deals specific to the scanned product.
- **RedLaser**: A reliable option for scanning barcodes and finding price comparisons at a variety of stores, both online and physical.
- **Amazon App**: Amazon's own app features a barcode scanner that allows you to check prices and availability within Amazon's inventory.

How to Use:

- Download and open the barcode scanning app of your choice.

- Point your phone's camera at the barcode and let the app scan it.
- Review the list of prices from different retailers and identify the lowest one.

2. Price Comparison Websites

Price comparison sites can be used before and during Black Friday to cross-check the price of a specific item across various retailers. These sites often have search functions where you can type in a product name, model number, or SKU to find its price at different stores.

Top Price Comparison Sites:

- **Google Shopping**: A comprehensive tool that aggregates prices from thousands of online stores. It also allows you to filter results by price, brand, and seller rating.
- **PriceGrabber**: This site is excellent for comparing prices on a wide range of products, from electronics to home goods.
- **CamelCamelCamel**: Specifically for Amazon, this tool tracks price history and alerts you when a product's price drops below a certain level.

How to Use:

- Go to the price comparison site and type in the name of the product or its model number.
- Browse the list of current prices and check for additional details like shipping costs and seller ratings.
- Bookmark these sites or keep them open during your shopping to make quick checks as needed.

Identifying Fake Discounts and Inflated "Regular" Prices

One of the most common marketing tactics used during Black Friday is inflating the original price of an item to make the discount appear more significant than it actually is. Understanding how to spot these fake discounts ensures you only invest in true savings.

1. Recognize the "Was" and "Now" Trap

Many retailers use labels that show a "was" price alongside a "now" price to emphasize the discount. However, the original "was" price may have been inflated or rarely used to make the discount seem larger.

How to Spot Inflated Prices:

- **Check Price History**: Use tools like CamelCamelCamel or Honey's price history feature to see if the "was" price was actually used for an extended period or if it was a marketing gimmick.
- **Compare with Other Retailers**: If multiple stores are selling the same product, look at how they present the original price. If most show a lower regular price, the "was" price on the initial site is likely exaggerated.

2. Beware of Limited-Time Hype

Countdown timers and "only a few left" messages are designed to create a sense of urgency. While some deals are genuinely limited, this tactic can be misleading and push you into making a hasty decision.

Steps to Verify:

- **Cross-Check with Competitor Sites**: See if the same product is listed at a similar "limited-time" discount elsewhere.
- **Check Price Tracking Data**: Use apps or extensions that show you how long a product has been at its current price to determine if the urgency is warranted.

3. Analyze "Special Buy" or "Black Friday Edition" Labels

Products labeled as "special buys" or "Black Friday editions" are often made specifically for sales events and may have fewer features or lower-quality components compared to their standard counterparts.

How to Identify:

- **Read the Product Description Carefully**: Compare the specifications of the "special buy" item with those of the standard model.
- **Look for Reviews**: Check online reviews for the specific version being sold. If there are limited reviews or none at all, proceed with caution.
- **Consult Forums**: Online forums and deal sites may have discussions about specific "Black Friday edition" products and whether they're worth purchasing.

Leveraging Price Match Guarantees

Price match guarantees are policies that allow you to get a refund for the price difference if you find an item you purchased at a lower price at another store or even the same store within a certain period. Knowing how to take advantage of these guarantees can amplify your savings during Black Friday.

1. Understand Store Policies

Not all stores have the same price match policies, and they may change during Black Friday or other major sales events. Review the price match policies of your preferred retailers before shopping.

Common Price Match Policy Points:

- **Eligible Items**: Some stores only match prices on identical items, including model numbers and brand names.
- **Competitor Matches**: Certain retailers only match prices from a pre-approved list of competitors.
- **Exclusions**: Many stores exclude Black Friday and Cyber Monday deals from their price match policies, so check for any fine print or disclaimers.

Examples:

- **Best Buy**: Typically has a robust price match policy, but often excludes special sales like Black Friday.
- **Target**: Offers price matching with select competitors and its own website.
- **Walmart**: May offer limited price matching but can vary by store location.

2. Document Your Evidence

If you plan to request a price match, have your evidence ready. This can include screenshots of the competitor's price, printed ads, or links to product pages.

Tips for Evidence Collection:

- **Take Timely Screenshots**: Online prices can change quickly, so take screenshots as soon as you see a lower price.
- **Keep Ads and Flyers**: If a local store advertises a lower price, save the flyer or ad as proof.

3. Timing Your Price Match Request

Timing is crucial when requesting a price match. Some stores only allow price matches at the time of purchase, while others offer a grace period (e.g., 7-14 days) after purchase for price adjustments.

Strategies:

- **Same-Day Price Match**: Request a price match at the time of purchase if you find a lower price on the same day.
- **Post-Purchase Price Adjustment**: Monitor the prices of high-value items you bought for up to two weeks after Black Friday to see if you can request a post-purchase adjustment.

4. Use Price Matching to Your Advantage During Pre-Black Friday Sales

Many stores start rolling out deals before Black Friday. If you make a purchase early and notice a better deal on the same item on Black Friday, use the price match policy to get the lower price without having to return the item and rebuy it.

Pro Tip: Confirm with the retailer's customer service that pre-Black Friday purchases are eligible for price matching during the main event to avoid surprises.

5. Prepare for Negotiation

Sometimes, obtaining a price match involves negotiation with store associates or customer service representatives. Be polite but firm, and have your evidence readily available.

Negotiation Tips:

- **Stay Informed**: Know the store's policy details so you can reference them if needed.
- **Be Persistent**: If the first associate declines your request, politely ask to speak with a manager who may have more authority to approve the price match.
- **Be Flexible**: If a store offers store credit or a gift card instead of a price match refund, consider accepting it if you plan to shop there again.

Final Thoughts

Advanced price comparison techniques are an essential part of maximizing your savings during Black Friday. By using barcode scanners and price comparison sites, identifying fake discounts, and leveraging price match guarantees, you can shop confidently, knowing you are getting the best possible deals. These strategies will empower you to distinguish between true bargains and marketing gimmicks, making your Black Friday shopping experience more efficient and rewarding.

Chapter 9: Coupon Stacking and Discount Combinations

When it comes to Black Friday shopping, understanding how to maximize savings goes beyond just looking for advertised discounts. Knowing how to stack coupons and take advantage of various discount combinations can result in significant cost savings. This chapter will provide an in-depth look at understanding store policies on coupons, utilizing digital coupon apps and loyalty programs, and leveraging store credit cards and promotions to maximize your savings.

Understanding Store Policies on Coupons and Stacking

Before attempting to stack coupons or combine different discounts, it's crucial to understand the policies of the stores where you plan to shop. Each retailer has its own rules about how discounts and promotions can be applied.

1. Types of Coupons and Their Restrictions

Coupons come in various forms, such as manufacturer coupons, store coupons, and promo codes. It's important to know which types can be combined and which cannot.

Types of Coupons:

- **Manufacturer Coupons**: Issued by the product's manufacturer and can often be combined with store coupons.
- **Store Coupons**: Issued by the retailer and may have restrictions about stacking with other store-issued discounts.
- **Promo Codes**: Online codes that can apply to your cart at checkout. Some can be stacked with other offers, while others cannot.

Common Restrictions:

- **Single-Use Limitations**: Some coupons may be used only once per transaction or per customer.
- **Non-Stackable Codes**: Certain promo codes may not be combined with other discounts or offers.

- **Exclusion Clauses**: High-demand items, electronics, or specific brands may be excluded from coupon usage.

2. Coupon Stacking Policies

Not all stores allow coupon stacking, so it's vital to check each store's policy beforehand. Coupon stacking refers to the ability to apply more than one coupon or promo code to a single purchase, increasing overall savings.

Examples of Store Policies:

- **Target**: Typically allows one manufacturer coupon and one store coupon per item. You can also use the Target Circle app to stack additional discounts.
- **Kohl's**: Often allows customers to use Kohl's Cash, percentage-off coupons, and promo codes together for substantial savings.
- **CVS**: Offers ExtraBucks rewards that can be used with coupons for even greater savings.

Steps to Check Policies:

- Visit the store's website and review the coupon policy under the "FAQs" or "Customer Service" sections.
- Call or visit the store in advance to confirm coupon stacking rules with a store associate.

Digital Coupon Apps and Loyalty Programs

The rise of digital shopping has made it easier than ever to find and apply coupons through apps and loyalty programs. These tools can help you organize your coupons and maximize savings with minimal effort.

1. Must-Have Digital Coupon Apps

Digital coupon apps streamline the process of finding and applying coupons, making it easy to save on-the-go.

Top Coupon Apps:

- **Honey**: Automatically finds and applies the best promo codes at checkout for online purchases.
- **RetailMeNot**: Offers a wide range of online and in-store coupons and cashback deals.
- **Coupons.com**: Provides manufacturer coupons that can be printed or applied directly to your store loyalty card for easy redemption.

How to Use These Apps:

- **Download and Sign Up**: Install the app and create an account.
- **Search for Coupons**: Look up coupons for your preferred stores or products.
- **Apply Coupons**: Follow the app's instructions to apply the coupons in-store or during online checkout.

2. Loyalty Programs for Additional Savings

Many retailers offer loyalty programs that reward customers with points, discounts, or exclusive coupons. Joining these programs can enhance your savings when combined with other discounts.

Examples of Loyalty Programs:

- **Target Circle**: Offers exclusive coupons and 1% cashback on purchases. Can be stacked with other discounts and coupons.
- **Walgreens Balance Rewards**: Provides points for purchases that can be redeemed for store credit.
- **Macy's Star Rewards**: Grants members exclusive discounts and points for every dollar spent, which can later be redeemed for savings.

Tips for Maximizing Loyalty Programs:

- **Sign Up Early**: Ensure you're registered for loyalty programs well before Black Friday to take advantage of member-only deals.
- **Link Your Accounts**: Connect your loyalty account to the store's app for easier access to deals and digital coupons.
- **Monitor Special Events**: Some stores offer double or triple points days, which are ideal for making larger purchases.

3. Cashback Apps and Rebates

Cashback apps like Rakuten and Ibotta can be combined with coupons and loyalty programs to further boost savings.

Using Cashback Apps:

- **Rakuten**: Sign up for Rakuten and use the app or browser extension to activate cashback before making a purchase. Cashback accumulates and is paid out quarterly.
- **Ibotta**: Offers rebates on groceries and other purchases. Simply select the items you're buying, scan your receipt, and earn cashback.

Pro Tip: Combine cashback offers with loyalty points and coupons for maximum savings. For instance, use a coupon app to apply discounts, pay with a store credit card that offers points, and activate a cashback offer through Rakuten.

Maximizing Savings with Store Credit Cards and Promotions

Store credit cards can be powerful tools for maximizing Black Friday savings when used strategically. These cards often offer exclusive promotions, discounts, and rewards that can be combined with other savings methods.

1. Store Credit Card Perks

Retailers often provide special incentives for cardholders, such as early access to sales, additional percentage-off discounts, or rewards points that accumulate with every purchase.

Examples of Store Card Benefits:

- **Target RedCard**: Offers 5% off every purchase, free shipping on most items, and extended return periods.
- **Macy's Credit Card**: Provides Star Money Days where cardholders earn extra points that can be redeemed for store credit.
- **Amazon Store Card**: Offers 5% cashback on Amazon purchases for Prime members and special financing options.

Considerations Before Applying:

- **Interest Rates**: Store credit cards often come with high-interest rates, so pay off balances in full to avoid interest charges.
- **Spending Limits**: Be mindful of spending limits and avoid overspending just to earn rewards.
- **Credit Impact**: Applying for new credit can impact your credit score, so ensure that it aligns with your financial goals.

2. Combining Credit Card Promotions with Coupons

Many stores allow cardholders to use their credit card discounts in conjunction with store coupons and promotions.

Example Strategy:

- Use a 20% off store coupon.
- Apply a store credit card discount (e.g., 5% off).
- Add loyalty points earned from the purchase.
- Activate cashback through a site like Rakuten for additional savings.

3. Watch for Special Cardholder Events

Some stores hold special sales events or offer additional perks exclusively for cardholders during Black Friday.

Tips for Cardholder Events:

- **Sign Up for Alerts**: Subscribe to email or text alerts from your store credit card to be notified of cardholder-exclusive deals.
- **Plan Your Purchases**: Save high-value items for cardholder event days when discounts and rewards are higher.
- **Use Cardholder-Only Coupons**: Check for coupons or promo codes that are only available to store cardholders.

Final Thoughts

Coupon stacking and discount combinations can significantly reduce your total spending during Black Friday, but only if you understand how to navigate store policies and utilize the right tools. By learning the art of combining digital coupons, loyalty program benefits, and store credit card promotions, you'll maximize your savings and make your Black Friday shopping more efficient and rewarding. With careful preparation, you'll be well-equipped to navigate complex discount structures and come out ahead with substantial savings.

Chapter 10: Mastering the Art of Negotiation

Negotiation is an often-overlooked aspect of shopping, especially during sales events like Black Friday when deals seem fixed and non-negotiable. However, mastering negotiation techniques can lead to substantial savings, especially on big-ticket items. This chapter will guide you through effective ways to negotiate discounts, communicate with customer service for additional perks, and use insider phrases and tactics that yield real results.

Effective Ways to Negotiate Discounts on Big-Ticket Items

Big-ticket items such as electronics, furniture, and appliances often carry price tags that seem inflexible, but savvy shoppers know that there is usually room for negotiation, even during sale periods like Black Friday. Here's how to approach negotiating these items effectively:

1. Do Your Homework

Research is crucial for successful negotiation. Know the current market value of the item, including its historical sale prices, competitor pricing, and typical markdowns during Black Friday.

Steps to Research:

- **Price Tracking Tools**: Use tools like CamelCamelCamel for Amazon items or Honey's price history feature to see if the current deal is truly the lowest.
- **Competitor Pricing**: Check similar items at different retailers and note down any price differences.
- **Specifications and Features**: Be well-versed in the specific features of the item to negotiate effectively if similar models with fewer features are cheaper elsewhere.

2. Use the Bundle Approach

Retailers are often more willing to offer a discount when you purchase multiple items together. Bundle your big-ticket item with smaller items or accessories to make a larger sale and potentially secure a better deal.

Example:

- If purchasing a new TV, negotiate for discounted soundbars, HDMI cables, or wall mounts as part of the package.
- For large appliances, ask for delivery, installation, or extended warranties to be included at no extra charge.

3. Target Open-Box and Display Models

Big-ticket items that are open-box or display models can be significantly cheaper than their unopened counterparts. Retailers are typically eager to move these items, so don't hesitate to negotiate an even deeper discount.

Tips for Negotiating Open-Box Items:

- **Point Out Flaws**: Mention any visible scratches or wear to justify a price reduction.
- **Ask About Warranty**: Confirm if the warranty still applies to open-box items and use the lack of coverage as leverage for a lower price.
- **Offer to Pay Cash**: Some retailers may offer better prices for cash purchases, as it saves them credit card processing fees.

4. Timing is Key

Timing your negotiation can also impact its success. Sales associates and managers may be more inclined to negotiate at quieter times when there's less foot traffic and more time to engage with customers.

Best Times to Negotiate:

- **End of the Month/Quarter**: Sales targets may push associates to be more flexible with pricing.
- **Late Afternoon or Evenings**: When store managers are present, they often have more authority to approve discounts.

How to Communicate with Customer Service for Additional Perks

Approaching customer service with the right strategy can yield additional perks, such as free shipping, extended warranties, or exclusive discounts. It's all about building rapport and presenting your request in a professional, yet assertive manner.

1. Be Polite and Personable

Approach customer service interactions with a positive attitude. Staff members are more likely to help customers who are polite and respectful than those who are confrontational.

Tips for Building Rapport:

- **Use the Associate's Name**: People respond better when addressed by name. Read their name tag or ask for their name if speaking over the phone.
- **Start with Small Talk**: A brief, friendly comment can make the conversation more pleasant and open.

2. Ask Open-Ended Questions

Asking open-ended questions gives the associate an opportunity to offer solutions that you might not have considered.

Examples of Open-Ended Questions:

- "Is there any additional discount available for this item?"
- "What's the best price you could offer if I buy this today?"
- "Are there any upcoming promotions that might apply to this product?"

3. Mention Competitor Pricing

If you've found a better price elsewhere, bring it up during the conversation. Retailers don't want to lose a sale to a competitor, so they may be willing to match or even beat the competitor's price.

Key Points to Mention:

- **State the Competitor's Offer Clearly**: Be specific about where you saw the lower price and what it included.
- **Provide Proof**: Have a printout, ad, or website link ready to show the associate or send to customer service.

4. Inquire About Additional Perks

If a price match isn't possible, shift the conversation to other perks that could add value to your purchase.

Perks to Ask For:

- **Free or Discounted Shipping**: Especially valuable for large items.
- **Extended Warranty**: A common request for electronics or appliances.
- **Free Accessories**: Items like protective cases for electronics or extra cables can be added to sweeten the deal.

Insider Phrases and Tactics That Yield Results

The way you phrase your request can influence its success. Certain phrases signal that you are an informed shopper and may compel a store associate to be more flexible. Additionally, specific tactics can give you an edge in negotiating.

1. Use Value-Driven Language

Highlight the value you bring as a customer to the store or company, subtly suggesting that accommodating your request will benefit both parties.

Effective Phrases:

- "I'm very interested in this product but am weighing my options. Is there anything you can do to make this the best choice for me?"
- "I've seen similar items priced lower elsewhere, and I'd prefer to buy from here. Is there any way you can match that price?"
- "I'm a loyal customer and would love to continue shopping here if you can work with me on this."

2. Reference Past Promotions

Mentioning past discounts or promotions signals that you're aware of what the retailer is capable of offering and might prompt them to provide a comparable deal.

Example:

- "I remember that last year you offered a 15% discount on similar items during Black Friday. Is there any way we could do something similar today?"

3. Utilize the "Pause" Tactic

After making your request, pause and give the associate time to consider it. Silence can be powerful and may encourage the associate to fill it with an offer or solution.

How to Implement:

- State your request or counteroffer, then pause and maintain eye contact or wait patiently on the phone. Avoid filling the silence with additional justifications or explanations.

4. Be Prepared to Walk Away

One of the strongest negotiation tactics is being ready to walk away. If an associate sees that you're not desperate to make a purchase, they may offer a last-minute incentive to close the sale.

When to Use This Tactic:

- If you're close to agreeing on a price but need that final push to secure a better deal.
- When negotiating high-ticket items and the store is highly motivated to make the sale.

5. Speak to a Manager if Needed

If the associate is unable to meet your request, don't hesitate to ask for a manager. Managers often have more discretion to approve additional discounts or perks.

Example Request:

- "I understand that this may be outside of the standard policy, but could I speak to a manager to see if there's any flexibility?"

Final Thoughts

Negotiating can seem intimidating, but with the right approach and insider knowledge, you can secure better prices and added perks. Effective negotiation involves thorough research, confident communication, and strategic tactics to make your case compelling. By mastering these techniques, you can enhance your Black Friday shopping strategy, ensuring you not only find great deals but also walk away with the best possible price on your purchases.

Chapter 11: Strategizing with Friends and Family

Black Friday shopping can be an exhilarating yet challenging experience, especially when aiming to secure high-demand products and maximize savings. Strategizing with friends and family adds a team dynamic to the process, enhancing your chances of success. This chapter will explore how to create group shopping plans for high-demand products, share coupon codes and loyalty points effectively, and synchronize shopping times for shared purchases.

Creating Group Shopping Plans for High-Demand Products

High-demand products, such as limited edition electronics, luxury items, or exclusive deals, often sell out quickly. Forming a group shopping plan with friends or family can increase your chances of obtaining these sought-after products.

1. Assigning Roles and Responsibilities

One of the most effective strategies for group shopping is to assign specific roles and responsibilities to each member of your team. This division of labor ensures that everyone knows their tasks and minimizes duplication of efforts.

Role Examples:

- **Primary Buyer**: The person designated to make the actual purchase, with payment details pre-saved for quick checkout.
- **Deal Finder**: A member responsible for monitoring prices, checking stock availability, and alerting the team to new or updated deals.
- **Backup Shopper**: In case the primary buyer faces technical issues or fails to secure an item, the backup shopper steps in to make the purchase.
- **Store Scout**: If shopping in-store, assign someone to arrive early and secure a place in line while others monitor online sales.

Tips for Assigning Roles:

- Choose team members who are most comfortable with their roles (e.g., tech-savvy individuals for online monitoring).
- Ensure everyone has reliable communication tools, such as smartphones with messaging apps.

2. Creating a Coordinated Shopping List

Develop a master list of items that your group is targeting, complete with details such as product specifications, priority levels, and store locations.

Creating the List:

- Use shared digital tools like Google Sheets or Trello to list all items, prices, stores, and responsible individuals.
- Mark high-priority items and note which items are time-sensitive (e.g., part of flash sales).

List Structure Example:

Item	Store	Priority Level	Buyer	Time Slot
4K Smart TV	Best Buy	High	Alex	Midnight
Gaming Laptop	Amazon	High	Sarah	Early Morning
Designer Watch	Macy's	Medium	Daniel	Afternoon

3. Synchronizing Communication

Maintain clear communication channels to update each other on the status of purchases and stock changes.

Communication Tools:

- **Group Chat Apps**: Use apps like WhatsApp, Signal, or a group text thread for instant updates.
- **Real-Time Collaboration Platforms**: Platforms like Slack or Discord can organize discussions into specific channels (e.g., "Electronics" or "Flash Sales").

Pro Tip: Use shorthand codes for updates (e.g., "TV – Got it!" or "Laptop – OOS (out of stock)") to save time.

Sharing Coupon Codes and Loyalty Points

Sharing resources like coupon codes and loyalty points among team members can significantly increase savings. Here's how to do it effectively:

1. Pooling Coupon Codes

Coordinate with your group to share and pool coupon codes that can be applied to purchases. This strategy ensures that everyone benefits from the best available discounts.

How to Share Codes:

- Create a shared document or chat thread where everyone can post usable coupon codes.
- Use platforms like Honey or RetailMeNot to find codes that may apply to multiple purchases.
- Ensure that members understand the rules for each code (e.g., single-use, store-specific).

2. Utilizing Shared Loyalty Accounts

Loyalty programs often allow family sharing or account linking to pool points for larger discounts.

Programs that Support Sharing:

- **Target Circle**: Allows points accumulation that can be used across multiple family accounts.
- **Macy's Star Rewards**: Points can be shared by using the same loyalty card at checkout.
- **Costco Membership**: Can be leveraged by members who share the same account for purchases.

Steps to Share Loyalty Benefits:

- Nominate one person to use the shared loyalty account for major purchases.

- Make sure everyone knows the account details needed to earn or redeem points (e.g., phone number or member ID).

3. Synchronizing Coupon Usage

When using single-use codes or time-sensitive coupons, coordination is key to ensure that codes are used strategically.

Example Strategy:

- Assign specific codes to team members based on the items they are buying.
- Prioritize the use of codes that provide the highest percentage savings for big-ticket items.
- Keep track of used codes in a shared document to avoid confusion.

Synchronizing Shopping Times for Shared Purchases

Coordinating when and where your group shops can help you secure popular items faster and more efficiently. Synchronizing shopping times also prevents overlapping efforts and reduces the chance of missing deals.

1. Planning Time Slots for Different Purchases

Create a timeline that outlines when each member will shop for specific items. This structured approach prevents conflicts and ensures that everyone is focused on different targets at various times.

Timeline Example:

- **12:00 AM – 3:00 AM**: Online purchases for electronics (Alex and Sarah).
- **3:00 AM – 6:00 AM**: Shift focus to online apparel and accessories (Mia and Daniel).
- **6:00 AM – 9:00 AM**: In-store purchases and backup online shopping (Group effort).

2. Setting Up Alert Systems

Use alert systems and app notifications to synchronize shopping activities. Each team member should be set up with alerts that inform them when deals go live or when stock is available.

Alert Tools:

- **Push Notifications**: Enable on retailer apps and deal-tracking platforms.
- **SMS Alerts**: Sign up for store-specific alerts that notify you of flash sales.
- **Email Updates**: Keep an eye on retailer newsletters for exclusive early-bird access links.

3. Coordinating Early Access and Exclusive Sales

Many retailers offer early access to sales for loyalty members or credit cardholders. Identify which members have these privileges and coordinate purchases accordingly.

How to Leverage Early Access:

- If a team member has a store credit card with early access perks, assign them to secure high-priority items during that window.
- Coordinate with store policies on early bird hours or member-only sale times to maximize your team's shopping efficiency.

4. Managing Checkout Overlaps

To avoid purchasing the same item twice or facing sold-out scenarios, communicate when an item has been secured by a team member.

Checkout Management Tips:

- **Update in Real Time**: Use your group chat or shared document to post when an item has been purchased (e.g., "TV – purchased by Sarah at 12:10 AM").
- **Confirm Before Proceeding**: Double-check with the group before checking out high-demand items.
- **Designate a Final Verifier**: Assign one person to confirm all items have been accounted for before everyone moves on to the next set of purchases.

Final Thoughts

Strategizing with friends and family can turn Black Friday shopping from a solo challenge into a coordinated, team-based event that maximizes your chances of securing high-demand items and getting the best deals. By creating group shopping plans, pooling resources like coupon codes and loyalty points, and synchronizing shopping times, you can tackle the frenzy of Black Friday with confidence and efficiency. The team approach not only enhances the shopping experience but ensures that everyone comes away with their targeted items and maximum savings.

Chapter 12: Leveraging Social Media for Flash Deals

In the digital age, social media has become a powerful tool for discovering and capitalizing on flash deals. Brands often use their social media channels to share exclusive promo codes, announce surprise sales, and engage directly with their customers. Joining online communities and using live streaming can further amplify your ability to stay ahead of the competition. This chapter will explore how to effectively leverage social media for Black Friday flash deals, including following brand accounts, joining shopper forums, and utilizing live streaming and alerts for flash sales.

Following Brand Accounts for Exclusive Promo Codes

Many brands and retailers use their social media accounts to communicate directly with their audience, offering followers exclusive access to deals and promo codes. Here's how to take advantage of this strategy:

1. Identify Key Accounts to Follow

Start by identifying the social media accounts of your favorite retailers and brands. Most major stores have active profiles on platforms like Instagram, Twitter, Facebook, and even TikTok, where they post special promotions and announcements.

Steps to Follow Brand Accounts:

- Search for official brand and retailer accounts on platforms like Instagram and Twitter.
- Follow not just the main account but also any regional or specific store accounts that may offer localized deals.
- Enable notifications for these accounts to receive instant updates when new posts or stories are shared.

Examples of Brands to Follow:

- **Electronics**: Best Buy, Newegg, Amazon, Target
- **Apparel**: Nike, H&M, Macy's, Old Navy
- **Home Goods**: Wayfair, IKEA, Home Depot

2. Monitor Social Media Stories and Reels

Brands often use short-lived content like stories or reels to post flash sales or promo codes that may only be active for a few hours. Make it a habit to check these sections regularly, especially during Black Friday week.

Tips for Monitoring Stories:

- Set reminders to check stories at the start of key shopping hours, such as early morning or midday.
- Swipe up or click on the links provided in stories for direct access to deals.
- Screenshot or save promo codes and use them at checkout before they expire.

3. Engage with the Content for Better Visibility

The algorithms on social media platforms prioritize accounts you engage with frequently. Like, share, and comment on posts from your preferred retailers to increase the likelihood of seeing their updates first in your feed.

Engagement Tips:

- Respond to questions or participate in polls in stories.
- Share brand posts with friends or in your own stories to spread awareness (and potentially get noticed by the brand for future giveaways).

Joining Shopper Forums and Online Deal Communities

Online communities and forums are valuable sources of real-time information and tips from other savvy shoppers. These platforms provide a space to share experiences, find exclusive promo codes, and discuss deals.

1. Popular Online Deal Communities

There are several well-established platforms where deal hunters gather to share and discuss the best deals available. Joining these communities can give you an edge by keeping you informed about flash sales and hard-to-find discounts.

Top Communities:

- **Reddit**: Subreddits like r/BlackFriday, r/deals, and r/frugal offer user-driven discussions and alerts about upcoming and live deals.
- **Slickdeals**: A dedicated website where users post and vote on deals. Slickdeals also has an app that provides instant alerts for user-selected categories.
- **DealNews**: A comprehensive site with deal postings and analysis on a wide range of products.

How to Get the Most Out of These Communities:

- Join relevant subreddits and enable notifications for keywords related to your shopping list.
- Participate in discussions to ask questions about product quality, delivery times, and the legitimacy of deals.
- Subscribe to email newsletters or daily deal summaries from these platforms for curated updates.

2. Use Social Media Groups

Facebook and other platforms host groups dedicated to deal hunting, especially around major sales like Black Friday. These groups often share promo codes, early access links, and reviews.

Tips for Participating in Groups:

- Join both public and private groups with high activity rates.
- Use search functions within the group to find posts about specific products or stores.
- Contribute by sharing your own findings or asking questions about ongoing promotions.

3. Partner with Influencers and Bloggers

Some social media influencers and bloggers have partnerships with brands, giving them access to exclusive discount codes or early sale information. Following these individuals can provide additional savings opportunities.

How to Find Influencers:

- Search hashtags like #BlackFridayDeals, #SaleAlert, or #DealHunter to find influencers posting about current and upcoming promotions.
- Check the bio sections of influencers for affiliate links and promo codes.
- Follow niche-specific influencers who focus on areas relevant to your shopping list, such as tech, fashion, or home goods.

Live Streaming and Alerts for Flash Sales

Live streaming has become an innovative way for brands and influencers to showcase products and offer exclusive deals in real-time. Platforms like Instagram Live, Facebook Live, and YouTube are increasingly used for flash sale announcements and limited-time offers.

1. Tune into Brand Live Streams

Retailers often host live streaming events during Black Friday to highlight major deals, provide product demonstrations, and share exclusive promo codes.

Steps to Access Live Streams:

- Check the schedules for live events on brand pages a few days before Black Friday.
- Follow brands on platforms that support live streaming, such as Instagram, YouTube, or Facebook.
- Set up notifications so you don't miss the start of a stream.

What to Expect:

- **Exclusive Promo Codes**: Some brands may share codes or special links during the stream that aren't posted elsewhere.
- **Q&A Opportunities**: Use the live chat feature to ask questions about products or deals.
- **Instant Purchases**: Brands may include direct links to purchase featured items during the live event.

2. Use Alerts for Flash Sales

Flash sales are time-sensitive and can happen at any time during the Black Friday period. Setting up alerts ensures you are informed the moment a sale goes live.

Tools for Alerts:

- **Twitter Notifications**: Follow and set up alerts for deal-specific accounts like @Wario64 for gaming deals or @Deals for general promotions.
- **App Alerts**: Use deal apps like Slickdeals and Honey to set alerts for specific products or categories.
- **Google Alerts**: Create alerts for keywords like "flash sale Black Friday" or specific product names to get notifications directly to your email.

Tips for Managing Alerts:

- Prioritize alerts for high-priority items and major retailers.
- Use a dedicated email folder for deal alerts to keep your inbox organized and reduce distractions.

3. Watch Influencer Sales Streams

Many influencers host live shopping events where they review products and offer exclusive promo codes. These streams can be beneficial for getting honest reviews and unadvertised discounts.

How to Participate:

- Follow influencers who announce upcoming streams related to Black Friday.
- Have your payment details saved and ready to go, as flash sale codes may only be active for a short time.
- Use the live chat feature to ask about additional deals or clarifications on product details.

Final Thoughts

Leveraging social media for flash deals adds an exciting and effective dimension to your Black Friday shopping strategy. By following brand accounts for exclusive promo codes, joining shopper forums and deal communities, and participating in live streaming events and flash sale alerts, you'll stay ahead of the game and secure the best possible deals. With these strategies in place, your social media feeds become powerful tools in your Black Friday arsenal, keeping you informed, prepared, and ready to act when the perfect deal comes your way.

Chapter 13: Post-Black Friday Tips for Returns and Exchanges

After the frenzy of Black Friday shopping, you might find that some items don't meet your expectations or that you need to make exchanges. Navigating returns and exchanges can be tricky, especially when items are marked as "final sale" or when you've made purchases from multiple retailers. This chapter will cover how to manage return policies effectively, handle final sale items strategically, and keep track of receipts and orders for a smooth post-Black Friday experience.

Navigating Return Policies with Minimal Hassle

Understanding and adhering to return policies is crucial for stress-free exchanges and returns. Each retailer may have different rules, and knowing them can save you time and money.

1. Review Store Return Policies Before You Buy

Many retailers have specific return policies that differ for items bought during Black Friday or other major sales. Familiarize yourself with these policies in advance to avoid surprises.

Common Return Policy Details to Check:

- **Return Window**: The typical return period is 14-30 days, but it may be shorter for Black Friday purchases.
- **Condition Requirements**: Some stores only accept returns if the item is unopened and in its original packaging.
- **Proof of Purchase**: Most stores require a receipt or order confirmation for returns.

Where to Find This Information:

- Visit the retailer's website and look for their return policy under the "Customer Service" or "Help" section.
- Check emails and receipts that include return instructions specific to your purchase.

2. Understand Different Return Methods

Retailers may offer multiple return options, such as in-store, mail-in, or third-party services. Choose the method that's most convenient for you.

Return Methods:

- **In-Store Returns**: Often the fastest option, especially if the retailer has a physical location nearby.
- **Mail-In Returns**: Ensure you understand the process for obtaining a return label and whether shipping costs are covered.
- **Third-Party Returns**: Some retailers partner with services like Happy Returns or UPS Drop Off, simplifying the return process.

Tips for In-Store Returns:

- Visit the store during non-peak hours to avoid long lines.
- Bring a valid ID and the original form of payment for faster processing.

3. Handle Return Shipping Costs Wisely

Return shipping fees can sometimes offset the value of returning an item. Before sending anything back, check if the retailer covers return shipping.

Strategies to Minimize Shipping Costs:

- **Free Return Labels**: Some retailers, like Amazon, offer free return labels for certain items. Verify if your purchase qualifies.
- **Use Membership Perks**: Programs like Amazon Prime and Target's RedCard often include free returns as part of their benefits.
- **Consolidate Returns**: If possible, combine multiple returns into a single shipment to save on shipping costs.

How to Handle "Final Sale" Items Strategically

"Final sale" items can be tricky, as they're often non-returnable or come with stricter rules. However, there are strategies for handling these purchases effectively.

1. Double-Check Item Details Before Buying

When shopping for items marked as final sale, take extra precautions to ensure they meet your needs.

Tips for Assessing Final Sale Items:

- **Read Product Descriptions Carefully**: Confirm sizes, dimensions, and specifications before buying.
- **Check Customer Reviews**: Look for insights on quality and fit from other buyers.
- **Ask Questions**: If you're uncertain about an item, reach out to the retailer's customer service before purchasing.

2. Selling or Exchanging Final Sale Items

If you end up with a final sale item you don't want, consider alternative methods to recover your investment.

Options for Unwanted Final Sale Items:

- **Resale Platforms**: List the item on resale sites like eBay, Poshmark, or Facebook Marketplace to recoup some of the cost.
- **Gift or Trade**: Offer the item to friends or family members who may need it, or trade for something you value.
- **Store Credit**: Some retailers may offer store credit instead of a refund, even for final sale items. It's worth asking.

3. Utilize Store Policies on Defective Products

If a final sale item is defective, retailers may be required to replace or repair it. Even if the item is marked as non-returnable, reach out to customer service if you discover a defect.

Steps for Handling Defective Final Sale Items:

- **Document the Issue**: Take clear photos or videos of the defect.
- **Contact Customer Service**: Be prepared to explain the issue and provide your receipt and evidence.
- **Request Replacement or Repair**: Many stores will offer a solution to maintain customer satisfaction.

Tips for Keeping Receipts and Tracking Orders

Keeping your receipts and tracking your orders are crucial for managing returns, exchanges, and warranty claims. Here's how to stay organized:

1. Organize Physical and Digital Receipts

Receipts are often required for returns and exchanges, so keep them secure.

Methods for Receipt Organization:

- **Physical Receipts**: Store in a dedicated folder or envelope, labeled by retailer or purchase date.
- **Digital Receipts**: Create a folder in your email inbox specifically for order confirmations and receipts. Use labels or tags to differentiate between stores.

Pro Tip: Take photos of physical receipts as a backup and store them in a cloud service or app like Evernote or Google Drive.

2. Use Apps for Digital Receipts and Order Tracking

Several apps can help keep your receipts and order details in one place, making it easier to track purchases and initiate returns.

Top Apps for Receipt and Order Management:

- **Expensify**: Perfect for scanning and storing receipts digitally.
- **Slice**: Automatically tracks your online orders and provides shipment updates.
- **Shopify App**: If you purchase from Shopify stores, this app tracks orders and sends notifications.

Tips for Using Apps:

- Connect your email or account to the app to allow it to scan for purchase confirmations.
- Set reminders for return deadlines within the app to avoid missing return windows.

3. Monitor Return Deadlines and Warranties

Ensure you know the return deadlines for each purchase, as Black Friday items may have different return policies than regular items.

How to Track Deadlines:

- **Create Calendar Reminders**: Use digital calendars to set reminders a few days before the return period ends.
- **Label Receipts**: If storing receipts physically, write the return deadline on each one.
- **Warranty Tracking**: If a product has a warranty, store the warranty details with your receipt for easy reference in case of future issues.

4. Maintain a Return Log

Keep a simple log of all items you plan to return, including the purchase date, store, receipt location, and return deadline.

Example Return Log:

Item	Store	Purchase Date	Return Deadline	Receipt Location	Status
Bluetooth Speaker	Best Buy	Nov 24	Dec 10	Email folder	Pending
Winter Jacket	Macy's	Nov 25	Dec 15	Envelope #1	Returned
Kitche n Blender	Amazon	Nov 26	Jan 5	Amazon Orders Page	Completed

5. Stay Proactive with Order Tracking

For online purchases, tracking your order's delivery status is essential to catch any potential issues early, such as delayed shipping or damaged items.

Steps for Tracking Orders:

- **Sign Up for Notifications**: Enable shipping updates from retailers or third-party apps like Shop or Arrive.
- **Keep Order Numbers Handy**: Save order confirmation emails and reference numbers to expedite customer service inquiries if needed.
- **Check Order Status Regularly**: Monitor tracking pages or carrier websites to ensure timely delivery.

Final Thoughts

Handling post-Black Friday returns and exchanges efficiently requires preparation, attention to detail, and a proactive approach. By understanding return policies, managing final sale items strategically, and organizing receipts and orders, you can ensure that your post-Black Friday experience is as smooth as possible. These tips not only help you navigate potential challenges but also protect your investment and maintain the value of your Black Friday finds.

Chapter 14: Avoiding Scams and Keeping Your Data Safe

The excitement of Black Friday shopping brings with it an increase in scams and cybersecurity threats. Cybercriminals often take advantage of major sales events to target unsuspecting shoppers with fraudulent sites, phishing emails, and unsecured payment methods. This chapter will guide you through recognizing signs of scams, using secure payment methods, and enhancing your cybersecurity practices to ensure a safe and successful Black Friday shopping experience.

Recognizing Signs of Fraudulent Sites and Offers

One of the most common tactics employed by cybercriminals during major sales events is the creation of fraudulent websites and fake offers. Recognizing these scams is the first step to protecting yourself and your finances.

1. Check the URL for Security Indicators

A secure website should always have certain characteristics in its URL and browser settings.

Signs of a Secure Website:

- **"https" Prefix**: Ensure the URL starts with "https" rather than "http," indicating the use of encryption for data security.
- **Padlock Icon**: Look for a small padlock icon in the address bar. Clicking on it should provide details about the site's security certificate.
- **Correct Domain Name**: Be wary of sites that use slight misspellings of well-known retailers (e.g., "amaz0n.com" instead of "amazon.com").

2. Analyze the Website's Design and Content

Fraudulent sites often have design flaws and inconsistencies that distinguish them from legitimate websites.

Red Flags to Watch For:

- **Poor Grammar and Spelling**: Genuine retailers rarely have spelling and grammatical errors on their sites.
- **Low-Quality Images**: Blurry or low-resolution images of products are often a sign of a scam.
- **Lack of Contact Information**: Authentic sites provide contact details, including customer service numbers and physical addresses.

3. Beware of Deals That Are Too Good to Be True

If a deal seems unusually generous or out of line with other retailers, it could be a scam designed to lure you into making a purchase or divulging your personal information.

Examples of Suspicious Deals:

- Offers that claim 90% off high-ticket items like luxury electronics or designer apparel.
- Free gift card promotions that require you to enter sensitive information to claim them.

How to Verify:

- Compare the deal with other reputable retailers. If no one else is offering a similar discount, be cautious.
- Run a quick search on scam reporting sites or forums to check if other users have flagged the site or deal as fraudulent.

Using Secure Payment Methods for Online Transactions

How you choose to pay online can greatly impact your safety. Certain payment methods offer better security and fraud protection than others.

1. Use Credit Cards Over Debit Cards

Credit cards generally offer stronger fraud protection than debit cards, minimizing your liability if your information is compromised.

Advantages of Credit Cards:

- **Fraud Protection**: Most credit card companies have zero-liability policies for fraudulent transactions.
- **Purchase Disputes**: Credit cards make it easier to dispute unauthorized or incorrect charges.
- **No Direct Link to Bank Account**: Using a credit card ensures that your bank balance is not immediately impacted if fraud occurs.

2. Enable Two-Factor Authentication (2FA)

Wherever possible, enable two-factor authentication for payment accounts like PayPal or digital wallets. This adds an additional layer of security by requiring a second form of verification.

How to Enable 2FA:

- Log into your account settings for your payment platform.
- Find the security section and choose 2FA options, such as receiving a code via text message or using an authentication app.
- Follow the prompts to set up 2FA.

3. Use Digital Wallets and Payment Apps

Platforms like PayPal, Apple Pay, and Google Pay add layers of encryption and prevent retailers from accessing your card details directly.

Benefits of Digital Wallets:

- **Encryption**: Your card details are encrypted and stored securely.
- **Tokenization**: Unique, one-time transaction codes are generated for each purchase, protecting your actual card number.
- **Ease of Use**: One-tap payment methods streamline checkout while enhancing security.

Pro Tip: Always update your digital wallet app and payment platform software to the latest version to ensure optimal security.

4. Avoid Direct Bank Transfers

Bank transfers and payment methods like Western Union are often non-reversible and should be avoided when shopping online. Use them only for trusted, high-value purchases when absolutely necessary.

Enhancing Cybersecurity for Safe Shopping

Improving your overall cybersecurity is key to safeguarding your data and ensuring a worry-free shopping experience. Here are advanced measures to consider:

1. Strengthen Your Passwords

Weak passwords are one of the primary reasons for compromised accounts. Ensure your passwords are strong and unique for each shopping or payment account.

Creating Strong Passwords:

- **Length and Complexity**: Use passwords that are at least 12 characters long and include a mix of letters, numbers, and special symbols.
- **Avoid Personal Information**: Don't use easily guessed information like birthdates, names, or common phrases.
- **Password Managers**: Use a password manager like LastPass or 1Password to generate and store complex passwords securely.

2. Keep Your Devices and Software Updated

Updates often contain security patches that protect against vulnerabilities exploited by hackers. Ensure all devices you use for online shopping are up-to-date.

Checklist for Device Security:

- **Operating System**: Update to the latest version on all devices.
- **Browsers**: Use the most recent version of your preferred browser to benefit from the latest security features.
- **Apps**: Ensure all shopping, payment, and deal-finder apps are current.

3. Use a Virtual Private Network (VPN)

A VPN encrypts your internet connection and hides your IP address, making it more difficult for hackers to intercept your data. This is especially important when shopping from public Wi-Fi networks.

Top VPN Recommendations:

- **NordVPN**: Known for its strong encryption and user-friendly interface.
- **ExpressVPN**: Offers high-speed connections and robust security features.
- **CyberGhost**: Ideal for beginners looking for a straightforward, secure VPN solution.

How to Use a VPN for Shopping:

- Install the VPN app on your device.
- Select a secure server location and connect.
- Begin your online shopping session with the added layer of protection.

4. Watch for Phishing Emails and Texts

Scammers often send fake emails or texts that appear to be from legitimate retailers, tricking recipients into clicking malicious links or providing personal information.

How to Identify Phishing Attempts:

- **Suspicious Links**: Hover over links without clicking to see the actual URL.
- **Urgency and Threats**: Be cautious of messages that pressure you to act immediately (e.g., "Your account will be locked unless you confirm your information now!").

- **Check Sender Details**: Verify that the sender's email address matches the official domain of the retailer (e.g., support@store.com vs. support@store-sales.info).

5. Secure Your Home Wi-Fi Network

Ensure your home network is secured, as an unsecured network can be an easy target for hackers.

Steps to Secure Your Network:

- **Change Default Router Passwords**: Use a strong, unique password for your router.
- **Enable WPA3 Encryption**: This is the latest and most secure encryption standard for Wi-Fi networks.
- **Disable Remote Management**: This prevents access to your router settings from external locations.

6. Monitor Your Financial Accounts Regularly

Keep an eye on your bank and credit card statements for any unauthorized transactions. Early detection is crucial for mitigating fraud.

Tips for Monitoring:

- **Set Up Alerts**: Many banks and credit card companies allow you to set transaction alerts for purchases over a specific amount.
- **Review Statements**: Check your account statements regularly for discrepancies or unfamiliar charges.
- **Act Quickly**: If you spot a fraudulent charge, contact your bank or credit card issuer immediately to report it and request a freeze on the account if necessary.

Final Thoughts

Avoiding scams and keeping your data safe during Black Friday shopping requires vigilance and proactive measures. By recognizing fraudulent sites, using secure payment methods, and enhancing your overall cybersecurity, you can shop confidently without the worry of falling victim to scams. Implementing these practices ensures that your Black Friday shopping experience is not only successful in terms of deals but also secure and worry-free.

Chapter 15: Shopping for Gifts vs. Personal Items

Black Friday is a prime opportunity to buy gifts and personal items at significant discounts. However, the overwhelming number of deals can make it difficult to strike a balance between purchasing gifts for others and treating yourself. This chapter will guide you through prioritizing gift purchases, keeping personal splurges in check, and creating a "gift-first" shopping plan to make the most of your Black Friday shopping.

Prioritizing Gift Purchases with Broad Appeal

When shopping for gifts during Black Friday, prioritizing items with broad appeal ensures that you find meaningful presents without getting lost in the endless sea of deals.

1. Identify High-Impact Gifts

Start by identifying gifts that have the most impact—those that are thoughtful, useful, and well-received by recipients.

Categories of High-Impact Gifts:

- **Electronics**: Popular gadgets like wireless headphones, smartwatches, or tablets.
- **Home Goods**: Items such as cozy blankets, coffee makers, or multi-purpose kitchen tools.
- **Personal Care**: Spa sets, skincare products, or luxury grooming kits.
- **Toys and Games**: For children, trending toys or educational games are always popular choices.

How to Prioritize:

- **Make a List**: Write down everyone you plan to buy gifts for, along with a few ideas for each person. Rank the recipients based on who you need to prioritize (e.g., immediate family, close friends).

- **Set a Budget Per Person**: Determine how much you're willing to spend on each person to prevent overspending on any one gift.

2. Choose Gifts with Universal Appeal

Selecting gifts that are widely appreciated can make the decision-making process simpler and reduce the risk of buying something that might not be used.

Examples of Gifts with Broad Appeal:

- **Gift Cards**: Choose gift cards to popular stores, coffee shops, or online retailers for maximum flexibility.
- **Home Essentials**: Items like candles, throw pillows, or decorative kitchenware are practical yet thoughtful.
- **Tech Accessories**: Phone chargers, power banks, or Bluetooth speakers are useful to almost anyone.

Tips for Choosing Versatile Gifts:

- Opt for neutral colors and simple designs when choosing home items or personal accessories.
- Stay informed about trending products to find gifts that align with current interests.

3. Look for Gift Bundles and Sets

Bundled items or gift sets offer great value and are perfect for gifts with a "wow" factor. Many retailers offer exclusive holiday sets at discounted prices during Black Friday.

Advantages of Gift Bundles:

- **Cost Savings**: Bundles typically cost less than buying each item individually.
- **Ready-Made Presentation**: Many bundles are pre-packaged in attractive gift boxes, saving you time on wrapping.

- **Multiple Recipients**: Split up a larger bundle into smaller gifts for different people to maximize your budget.

What to Watch For: Ensure the bundle's contents are high-quality and not filled with excess filler items to inflate the perceived value.

Keeping Personal Splurges in Check

While Black Friday deals can be tempting, it's important to keep personal spending in check to avoid exceeding your budget. Here's how to balance gift shopping and personal splurges:

1. Set a Personal Budget Limit

Before you start shopping, allocate a specific portion of your total budget for personal items. This keeps impulse buying under control and ensures you don't compromise your gift budget.

How to Set a Limit:

- **Assess Your Total Budget**: Calculate how much you're comfortable spending overall.
- **Allocate Percentages**: Dedicate a certain percentage of your budget for gifts (e.g., 70%) and a smaller portion for personal splurges (e.g., 30%).
- **Stick to Your Limit**: Monitor your spending to avoid exceeding your pre-set personal budget.

2. Prioritize Needs Over Wants

When browsing deals, it's easy to get caught up in buying items simply because they're on sale. To keep personal purchases in check, focus on items you genuinely need or have planned to buy.

Questions to Ask Yourself:

- **Is this a planned purchase?** If the item was on your list before Black Friday, it's likely worth buying if the deal is good.
- **Will I use this item frequently?** Only buy items you'll use regularly to avoid buyer's remorse.

- **Is this deal truly worth it?** Compare the current deal with historical prices to determine if it's genuinely a good offer.

3. Limit "Just for Me" Browsing Time

It's easy to get swept up in shopping for yourself, so set boundaries on how much time you'll spend looking at personal items versus gift shopping.

How to Manage Time:

- **Designate Personal Browsing Blocks**: Schedule specific times during your shopping day to look for personal items, such as a 30-minute window in the evening after securing all your gifts.
- **Reward Yourself Strategically**: Use personal shopping as a reward after completing your gift list. This helps you focus on others first and use any leftover budget for yourself.

Creating a "Gift-First" Shopping Plan

A structured shopping plan that prioritizes gift purchases helps ensure that you take advantage of the best deals for your loved ones before splurging on personal items.

1. Start with Your Gift List

Make your gift list the foundation of your shopping plan. Include details such as recipient names, potential gifts, and where to find the best deals.

Detailed Gift Plan Template:

Recipient	Gift Idea	Store(s)	Budget	Priority Level
Mom	Luxury robe	Macy's, Target	$50-$75	High
Brother	Wireless earbuds	Best Buy, Amazon	$50-$100	High
Friend (Alex)	Coffee maker	Walmart, Wayfair	$40-$60	Medium
Niece	Educational toy	Target, Amazon	$20-$40	High

Tips:

- **Rank by Priority**: Shop for the highest-priority gifts first to ensure they don't sell out.
- **Plan Store Visits**: Map out which stores to visit in person and which items to buy online to save time and effort.

2. Shop in Phases

Organize your shopping into phases to help you stay focused and avoid impulse buying.

Phase Breakdown:

- **Phase 1: High-Priority Gifts**: Secure deals on high-demand items early in the day or as soon as sales go live.
- **Phase 2: Secondary Gifts and Stocking Stuffers**: Shop for medium-priority gifts and smaller items during less competitive hours.
- **Phase 3: Personal Splurges**: Allocate time at the end of your shopping day to browse for personal items with whatever remains of your budget.

3. Monitor Gift Deals Throughout the Day

Black Friday deals can change quickly, with flash sales and limited-time offers popping up throughout the day. Set alerts for specific items on your gift list to ensure you don't miss sudden price drops.

Tools for Monitoring:

- **Deal Tracking Apps**: Use apps like Slickdeals and Honey to monitor prices and get notified when specific items go on sale.
- **Retailer Notifications**: Enable notifications from retailer apps to receive instant alerts about new deals and promotions.

4. Review Your Purchases and Adjust as Needed

After completing your initial gift shopping, review your list and check off items you've secured. This allows you to reallocate your budget if needed and identify any gaps.

Review Process:

- **Cross-Check with Your Budget**: Ensure you're staying within your gift budget and adjust accordingly.

- **Double-Check Return Policies**: Confirm the return policies for your gift purchases in case any changes need to be made later.
- **Plan for Backup Gifts**: Have a few alternative gift options in mind if certain items are sold out or no longer on sale.

Final Thoughts

Balancing gift shopping and personal splurges during Black Friday can be challenging, but with careful planning, you can manage both effectively. Prioritizing gift purchases, setting clear budgets, and sticking to a "gift-first" shopping plan helps you make the most of your budget and ensure that loved ones receive thoughtful and meaningful presents. By organizing your approach and maintaining discipline, you can walk away from Black Friday with a well-rounded collection of gifts and a few personal treats without overspending.

Chapter 16: Scoring Deals on Major Appliances and Electronics

Black Friday is renowned for its substantial discounts on major appliances and electronics, making it the perfect opportunity to invest in high-ticket items. However, not all deals are created equal, and understanding when to buy and what to skip can save you from regrettable purchases. This chapter will provide expert recommendations on top brands and models, and detail the best timing for purchasing tech items to maximize your savings.

Knowing When to Buy and What to Skip on Black Friday

While Black Friday is known for deals, knowing which appliances and electronics to prioritize and which to avoid ensures you spend your money wisely.

1. Best Electronics to Buy on Black Friday

Certain categories of electronics consistently offer some of the most significant discounts during Black Friday.

Electronics to Prioritize:

- **TVs**: Black Friday is famous for doorbuster TV deals, including models from top brands such as Samsung, LG, and Sony. Look for 4K Ultra HD and OLED models, as these tend to have the best discounts.
- **Laptops**: Both budget-friendly and high-end laptops see significant markdowns. Brands like Dell, HP, Lenovo, and MacBook models often feature competitive prices.
- **Smart Home Devices**: Products like smart speakers, video doorbells, and smart displays from brands like Google Nest, Amazon Echo, and Ring are usually discounted.

- **Headphones and Earbuds**: Noise-cancelling headphones from brands such as Bose and Sony, and popular wireless earbuds like Apple AirPods and Samsung Galaxy Buds, often have great deals.
- **Gaming Consoles**: While major price cuts on current-generation consoles are rare, bundle deals with games and accessories are common.

2. Appliances Worth Buying on Black Friday

Major appliances are often deeply discounted, making Black Friday a great time to buy household essentials.

Appliances to Prioritize:

- **Refrigerators**: Brands like Whirlpool, LG, and Samsung often see substantial markdowns on mid-range and premium models.
- **Washing Machines and Dryers**: Washer-dryer pairs from brands like Maytag, GE, and Samsung are frequently featured in Black Friday sales.
- **Kitchen Appliances**: Look for discounts on items like microwaves, dishwashers, and ovens from brands like KitchenAid, Bosch, and GE.

3. Items to Skip on Black Friday

Not all deals are as enticing as they seem. Some products may be better purchased at other times of the year or might not be the best value during Black Friday.

Items to Consider Skipping:

- **Older Model TVs**: While they may have significant markdowns, older TV models might lack updated features and technology found in newer models.
- **Budget Laptops**: Deeply discounted laptops may come with outdated hardware or limited capabilities. Ensure you read the specifications carefully.

- **Home Appliances Without Warranty**: If a deal on a major appliance doesn't include a warranty, it's best to avoid it, as repairs and maintenance can offset any initial savings.
- **Niche Electronics**: Specialty items like high-end sound systems or niche gaming peripherals may not see as substantial discounts as general-use items.

Expert Recommendations for Top Brands and Models

Knowing which brands and models are most reliable helps you make the best decision when hunting for Black Friday deals.

1. Televisions

When shopping for a TV, choose models that offer a balance between price, features, and reliability.

Top Brands and Models:

- **LG OLED C-Series**: Known for superior picture quality and deep blacks, the C-Series from LG is often discounted during Black Friday and is worth investing in if you're looking for a high-end viewing experience.
- **Samsung QLED**: The Q80 and Q90 series offer excellent brightness and color accuracy. These models typically have strong discounts during Black Friday.
- **Sony BRAVIA X-Series**: Known for integrating excellent picture processing and smart features, Sony's mid to high-range models are ideal for movie buffs and gamers.

2. Laptops and Computers

Whether you need a device for work, gaming, or casual browsing, Black Friday has options for everyone.

Top Brands and Models:

- **MacBook Air (M-Series Chip)**: Apple's MacBook Air with the M1 or M2 chip offers incredible performance and battery life. Keep an eye on discounts at retailers like Best Buy and Amazon.
- **Dell XPS 13**: A perennial favorite for its sleek design and high performance, the Dell XPS 13 is often part of Black Friday sales.
- **HP Spectre x360**: Known for its versatility and premium build, the HP Spectre x360 convertible laptop is a solid choice for professionals.

- **Lenovo Legion 5**: A popular choice among gamers for its powerful performance at a reasonable price. This model frequently features in Black Friday sales.

3. Home Appliances

If you're looking to upgrade your home with new appliances, consider these top brands:

Top Brands and Models:

- **Samsung Family Hub Refrigerator**: Features a smart screen and Wi-Fi connectivity, perfect for modern kitchens.
- **GE Profile Series Washer and Dryer**: Known for reliability and innovative features like smart home integration.
- **Bosch 800 Series Dishwasher**: Consistently rated as one of the best dishwashers for its quiet operation and superior cleaning capabilities.

Pro Tip: When purchasing appliances, consider bundles that include additional perks like free delivery or extended warranties.

Timing Your Purchase for the Best Prices on Tech

Understanding the timing of Black Friday deals is critical to securing the best possible price on major appliances and electronics. Here's how to time your purchases strategically:

1. Watch for Early Black Friday Sales

Many retailers start rolling out deals in the weeks leading up to Black Friday. Monitor early sales to see if the item you're eyeing goes on sale before the main event.

Tips for Early Sales:

- **Sign Up for Newsletters**: Retailer newsletters often provide early access to sales and promo codes.
- **Check "Pre-Black Friday" Promotions**: Brands like Amazon, Target, and Walmart run "Black Friday Preview" sales with competitive pricing.

2. Take Advantage of Doorbuster Deals

Doorbusters are usually released at specific times on Black Friday and are designed to create excitement. These deals often have limited stock and go quickly, so plan ahead.

How to Secure Doorbuster Deals:

- **Set Alerts**: Use apps like Slickdeals or retailer-specific apps to set alerts for when doorbuster deals go live.
- **Prepare to Check Out Fast**: Save your payment and shipping details in advance to expedite the checkout process.
- **Use Multiple Devices**: Have a laptop, tablet, and smartphone ready to increase your chances of success.

3. Monitor Cyber Monday and Extended Sales

If you miss out on Black Friday, Cyber Monday and extended weekend sales often provide a second chance to snag deals. Electronics and tech products frequently see additional markdowns during these events.

Cyber Monday Tips:

- **Compare Prices**: Use price comparison tools like Google Shopping or PriceGrabber to ensure you're getting the best deal.
- **Check Stock Updates**: Items that sold out on Black Friday may be restocked for Cyber Monday.
- **Review Retailer Policies**: Some stores extend Black Friday prices through the weekend, giving you more time to make a purchase.

4. Keep an Eye on Post-Black Friday Deals

Some retailers, especially online stores, continue offering deals in the weeks following Black Friday. Keep monitoring prices for tech items you didn't purchase on the main sale day.

Tips for Post-Black Friday Shopping:

- **Look for Bundle Offers**: Post-Black Friday promotions often include bundle deals that can offer more value.
- **Sign Up for Waitlists**: If an item is out of stock, some retailers allow you to join a waitlist and alert you when the item is available again at a discount.

5. Use Price Matching to Your Advantage

If you buy an item and find it cheaper elsewhere during the Black Friday period, check if the store you purchased from offers a price match policy.

How to Use Price Matching:

- **Know the Policy**: Familiarize yourself with the store's price match rules before shopping.
- **Keep Your Receipts**: Ensure you have proof of purchase and the competing retailer's lower price as evidence.
- **Act Quickly**: Most price match policies have a limited window, so initiate the process as soon as you find a lower price.

Final Thoughts

Scoring deals on major appliances and electronics during Black Friday requires strategic planning and informed decision-making. By knowing which items to prioritize, understanding expert recommendations for the best brands and models, and timing your purchases effectively, you can make the most of the discounts and walk away with high-quality products at unbeatable prices. Remember, preparation and vigilance are key to maximizing your Black Friday savings on big-ticket items.

Chapter 17: Home Goods and Clothing Strategies

Home goods and clothing are popular Black Friday categories, but knowing when and how to shop can significantly impact your savings and satisfaction. Whether you're updating your wardrobe or revamping your living space, a strategic approach helps you maximize discounts and make well-informed decisions. This chapter will delve into understanding trends in fashion and home decor discounts, the best times to shop for seasonal clothing and essentials, and fitting room hacks for quick apparel decisions.

Understanding Trends in Fashion and Home Decor Discounts

Recognizing the patterns in fashion and home decor discounts during Black Friday helps you focus your shopping on items that offer the most value and highest savings.

1. Popular Fashion Trends During Black Friday

Black Friday is a prime time for retailers to offer deep discounts on current and past season fashion items. Understanding which categories typically see the best discounts can help guide your buying decisions.

Categories with Notable Discounts:

- **Winter Wear**: Coats, boots, and sweaters are highly discounted as retailers push seasonal items during peak buying periods.
- **Denim and Casual Wear**: Brands often discount jeans, T-shirts, and loungewear, making it a good time to stock up on basics.
- **Athleisure and Activewear**: Expect significant markdowns on leggings, hoodies, and sports bras from brands like Nike, Adidas, and Lululemon.
- **Luxury and Designer Fashion**: While high-end brands may not offer Black Friday deals directly, department stores and luxury retailers often discount designer items.

Tips for Fashion Shopping:

- **Shop for Basics**: Essentials like jeans, plain tees, and undergarments are often on sale and provide lasting value.
- **Focus on Staple Pieces**: Invest in classic items that won't go out of style quickly, like a quality trench coat or cashmere sweater.

2. Home Decor Trends and Discounts

Black Friday is also an excellent opportunity to purchase home goods, including furniture, decorative items, and practical home essentials.

Popular Home Goods Deals:

- **Furniture**: Look for discounts on sofas, chairs, and tables, especially from online retailers like Wayfair and Overstock.
- **Bedding and Linens**: Retailers often offer significant discounts on sheets, comforters, and mattress toppers.
- **Smart Home Devices**: Smart thermostats, lights, and speakers are usually bundled with discounts.
- **Kitchenware**: High-quality cookware, blenders, and stand mixers are popular items during Black Friday sales.

Decor Trends to Watch:

- **Minimalist Aesthetic**: Simple, clean designs in neutral colors tend to dominate home decor deals.
- **Sustainable Products**: Look for deals on eco-friendly items like organic cotton sheets or recycled material rugs.
- **Multifunctional Furniture**: Pieces like storage ottomans and sleeper sofas are often marked down during Black Friday.

Best Times to Shop for Seasonal Clothing and Essentials

Timing your purchases for clothing and home essentials can make a difference in the deals you find and the quality of items available.

1. Shopping Early in the Season

While Black Friday is known for steep discounts, shopping at the start of the sale can ensure that you get your preferred sizes and styles.

Why Shop Early:

- **Stock Availability**: Popular sizes and colors can sell out quickly, especially for seasonal items like winter coats and boots.
- **Exclusive Early Bird Offers**: Some retailers offer early-bird discounts for shoppers who start their purchases as soon as sales begin.

Strategies for Early Shopping:

- **Set Alerts**: Use retailer apps or deal-finding tools to notify you when specific clothing items go on sale.
- **Join Loyalty Programs**: Membership perks often include early access to sales and exclusive discounts.

2. Mid-Sale Shopping for Additional Discounts

Retailers may introduce additional promotions as Black Friday progresses, including deeper discounts or limited-time flash sales.

Best Times to Shop Mid-Sale:

- **Midday Updates**: Some retailers refresh their discounts around noon to attract lunchtime shoppers.
- **Second Wave of Deals**: Check back on Friday evening or over the weekend for restocked items or added promotions.

Pro Tip: Keep an eye on multi-day sales that extend through Cyber Monday, as these can sometimes include clothing and home essentials not featured on Black Friday.

3. Late-Season Clearance

If you're willing to wait, post-Black Friday clearance sales in December can offer even steeper discounts on seasonal clothing. However, stock may be limited, and popular items could be sold out.

When to Shop Clearance:

- **Late December**: The period between Christmas and New Year's often features markdowns on remaining winter items and home decor.

Utilizing Fitting Room Hacks for Quick Apparel Decisions

Shopping for clothing in-store during Black Friday can be hectic, with long lines and crowded fitting rooms. Employing fitting room hacks can help streamline the process and ensure you make quick, confident decisions.

1. Know Your Measurements and Sizing

Understanding your exact measurements can reduce the time spent trying on items and helps you make faster decisions.

Tips for Measuring:

- **Take Your Measurements at Home**: Use a soft measuring tape to measure your chest, waist, hips, and inseam before heading to the store.
- **Consult Sizing Charts**: Many retailers have sizing charts on their websites or in-store tags. Use your measurements to cross-check and select the right size.

2. Dress for Efficient Trying-On

Wear clothing that makes it easy to try on items quickly without having to fully undress.

Ideal Shopping Outfit:

- **Leggings or Slim-Fit Pants**: These allow you to easily try on dresses, skirts, and longer tops.
- **Tank Top or T-Shirt**: Perfect for trying on jackets, cardigans, and sweaters without taking off your shirt.
- **Slip-On Shoes**: Save time when trying on pants or skirts by avoiding laces or boots.

Pro Tip: Bring a belt to check how different pants or skirts fit with an accessory.

3. Try Multiple Sizes at Once

When possible, grab two sizes of an item to avoid making multiple trips to the fitting room. This tactic is especially useful for items with varying fits, such as jeans or fitted dresses.

How to Maximize Fitting Room Time:

- **Choose Your Priorities**: Only try on items that are high-priority or uncertain fits to save time.
- **Use Mirrors Strategically**: Fitting rooms are often limited, so try items in front of a communal mirror if necessary to speed up your decision-making.
- **Set a Timer**: Limit your time in the fitting room to five minutes per item to maintain momentum.

4. Visualize Outfits to Avoid Impulse Buys

Think about how each item will pair with clothes you already own. If you can't envision at least three different outfits using the item, consider leaving it behind.

Visualization Tips:

- **Picture Wardrobe Combinations**: Mentally match new clothing items with shoes, accessories, and other pieces at home.
- **Bring a Photo Reference**: Have pictures of your current wardrobe on your phone to remind you of what you already own and what will pair well with new purchases.

Final Thoughts

Strategizing your Black Friday shopping for home goods and clothing can help you make smart purchases that align with current trends and personal needs. By understanding the best times to shop, knowing which items to prioritize, and using fitting room hacks for quick decisions, you can make the most of the season's deals while avoiding unnecessary spending. With these strategies in place, you'll leave Black Friday with a collection of home and fashion items that you'll appreciate long after the sales have ended.

Chapter 18: Travel and Experience Deals

Black Friday isn't just about snagging deals on tangible products; it's also an excellent time to score discounts on travel, vacation packages, and experiences. Knowing how to navigate these offers can result in significant savings on your next adventure or memorable activity. This chapter will explore the strategies for booking vacation packages, finding hidden discounts on experiences and events, and understanding the fine print of non-tangible purchases to avoid potential pitfalls.

Booking Vacation Packages and Travel Deals During Black Friday

Vacation packages, flights, and hotel bookings are popular categories for Black Friday promotions. However, getting the most out of these deals requires a strategic approach.

1. Research and Prepare Ahead of Time

Travel companies and airlines often tease their Black Friday deals before the actual event. This gives you time to research potential destinations and identify the best deals.

Pre-Booking Checklist:

- **Choose Your Destinations**: Have a list of a few preferred travel destinations and compare the average prices for flights, accommodations, and packages.
- **Sign Up for Alerts**: Join mailing lists from airlines, travel agencies, and booking sites like Expedia, Booking.com, and Skyscanner to get early notifications of upcoming deals.
- **Set Price Alerts**: Use travel apps like Hopper and Kayak to set alerts for flights and hotel prices, ensuring you're notified as soon as prices drop.

Pro Tip: If possible, be flexible with your travel dates. Black Friday deals often apply to specific time frames, so being open to a range of dates increases your chances of finding great savings.

2. Target Bundled Vacation Packages

Bundled packages that include flights, accommodations, and even activities often provide the best value during Black Friday sales. These deals are typically offered by online travel agencies (OTAs) such as Expedia and Travelocity.

Benefits of Bundled Packages:

- **Cost Savings**: Bundling services can be cheaper than booking each component separately.
- **Convenience**: Booking an all-in-one package reduces the hassle of coordinating different parts of your trip.
- **Added Perks**: Bundles may come with extras such as free breakfast, airport transfers, or activity vouchers.

How to Find the Best Bundles:

- **Check OTA Websites**: Explore the "Deals" or "Offers" sections of travel sites to find Black Friday bundles.
- **Compare Multiple Sources**: Don't rely on one site; check a few travel booking platforms for the best offer.
- **Read Reviews**: Ensure that the bundled hotel or airline has good ratings to avoid surprises.

3. Booking Flights and Accommodations Separately

In some cases, booking flights and accommodations separately can yield better deals. Use Black Friday to secure flight deals and then book your hotel through promotions or loyalty points for added savings.

Tips for Flight Deals:

- **Look for Flash Sales**: Airlines may have flash sales on Black Friday or Cyber Monday, offering substantial discounts for a limited time.
- **Use Frequent Flyer Miles**: If you have airline miles or points, Black Friday promotions might offer additional discounts or bonus points for booking during the sale.

Tips for Hotel Deals:

- **Leverage Loyalty Programs**: Hotels often offer exclusive deals to loyalty program members.
- **Book Directly**: Booking directly through a hotel's website may include extra perks like free room upgrades or complimentary breakfast.

How to Find Hidden Discounts on Experiences and Events

Beyond flights and hotel stays, Black Friday is a prime time to find discounts on experiences such as theme park tickets, concerts, and local tours.

1. Search for Experience-Specific Platforms

Platforms dedicated to experiences and activities, like Groupon, Viator, and Airbnb Experiences, often have Black Friday deals that can be used for local and international activities.

Experience Categories to Look For:

- **Amusement Parks and Attractions**: Discounts on entry tickets to theme parks and popular attractions.
- **Concerts and Shows**: Ticket sellers like Ticketmaster and StubHub may offer discounts on event tickets.
- **Tours and Excursions**: Viator and GetYourGuide often have deals on guided tours, adventure sports, and unique local activities.

Finding the Best Experience Deals:

- **Check Multiple Platforms**: Compare prices and discounts across several experience platforms.
- **Look for Coupons and Codes**: Websites like RetailMeNot or Honey can help you find additional coupon codes for experience platforms.

2. Follow Travel and Event Accounts on Social Media

Brands and travel companies often post flash deals or exclusive promo codes on their social media channels. Following these accounts or turning on notifications can give you a competitive edge.

Where to Look:

- **Instagram and Twitter**: Brands may share quick, time-sensitive deals via stories or tweets.
- **Facebook Groups**: Join travel and event-focused groups where users share deals they find.

Pro Tip: Engage with posts from your favorite travel accounts. Social media algorithms often prioritize content from accounts you interact with, so you'll be more likely to see posts about flash sales.

3. Utilize Travel Agencies and Credit Card Partnerships

Travel agencies and credit card companies often partner with airlines and hotels to offer exclusive Black Friday deals to their clients.

How to Leverage These Partnerships:

- **Check Your Credit Card Benefits**: Many credit cards have travel partnerships that offer bonus points or discounts on bookings made through their portals.
- **Contact a Travel Agent**: Agencies sometimes have access to exclusive deals that aren't advertised to the general public.
- **Browse Member Portals**: If you're part of a membership program like Costco Travel, check their site for exclusive Black Friday travel deals.

Important Fine Print to Watch Out for on Non-Tangible Purchases

When purchasing travel and experiences during Black Friday, the fine print can contain crucial information that impacts the value and flexibility of your deal.

1. Understand Cancellation and Change Policies

Travel deals often come with strict cancellation policies or additional fees for changes. Be sure to understand these terms before booking.

Key Details to Check:

- **Refundability**: Confirm whether the booking is refundable or non-refundable.
- **Change Fees**: See if there are fees associated with changing the travel dates or guest names.
- **Cancellation Windows**: Some deals are only refundable if canceled within a certain number of days after booking.

Tips:

- Choose travel insurance if available, especially for international trips or high-value bookings.
- Book with flexible cancellation policies whenever possible to accommodate unforeseen changes.

2. Review Blackout Dates and Restrictions

Promotions on travel and experiences may come with blackout dates that limit when you can use your booking.

What to Watch For:

- **Seasonal Restrictions**: Many travel deals exclude peak travel dates like Christmas, New Year's Eve, and major holidays.
- **Day of the Week Limitations**: Some promotions only apply to weekday bookings or specific times of the year.

Pro Tip: Always check the calendar availability before purchasing to ensure the dates align with your plans.

3. Watch Out for Additional Fees

Travel and experience deals may have hidden fees that aren't immediately visible in the promotion.

Potential Fees:

- **Resort Fees**: Even if your hotel stay is discounted, additional resort fees may apply.
- **Service Charges**: Experience platforms might charge service fees that aren't included in the ticket price.
- **Taxes**: Ensure that taxes are included in the price or are reasonably expected when calculating the total cost.

4. Confirm Payment Terms and Installment Options

Some travel deals may require full payment upfront, while others allow for installment plans.

Payment Considerations:

- **Upfront Costs**: Know if you need to pay the entire amount upfront or if a deposit is enough to secure your booking.
- **Installment Plans**: Check if the travel company or platform offers payment plans and whether there are added interest fees.

Pro Tip: Use credit cards with travel rewards or cashback benefits when making large purchases to maximize your savings and benefits.

Final Thoughts

Black Friday can be an ideal time to secure travel and experience deals, but it's crucial to approach these purchases with careful planning and a keen eye for detail. By researching ahead, understanding the terms and conditions, and leveraging partnerships and hidden discounts, you can book unforgettable trips and activities at a fraction of the usual cost. With these strategies, you'll be able to plan your next adventure confidently, knowing that you're getting the best possible value.

Chapter 19: Following Up on Post-Black Friday Deals

The deals don't stop once Black Friday is over. Savvy shoppers know that the days and weeks following Black Friday can offer additional opportunities for savings. Cyber Monday and extended weekend sales, as well as other late-year events like "Green Monday," present further chances to capitalize on deals and discounts. This chapter will guide you through leveraging these post-Black Friday sales, understanding the significance of late-year promotions, and setting reminders for potential price drops.

Capitalizing on Cyber Monday and Extended Weekend Sales

Cyber Monday has evolved into one of the biggest online shopping days of the year, often rivaling or surpassing Black Friday in terms of discounts, particularly in the tech and electronics sectors. Understanding how to approach Cyber Monday and extended weekend sales can maximize your savings.

1. Planning Your Cyber Monday Strategy

Approaching Cyber Monday with a clear plan ensures you make the most of the available deals without getting overwhelmed.

Steps to Prepare:

- **Identify High-Priority Items**: Make a list of items you missed or weren't satisfied with during Black Friday and focus on finding them during Cyber Monday.
- **Compare Prices**: Use price comparison tools such as PriceGrabber, Google Shopping, and CamelCamelCamel to ensure that the discounts are genuine.
- **Check Store Policies**: Some retailers may offer better discounts or additional perks for online purchases on Cyber Monday.

Pro Tip: Set alerts for price drops on items you're interested in through tools like Honey or Keepa to stay informed when deals go live.

2. Shop for Tech and Electronics

While Black Friday often has great in-store deals, Cyber Monday is the time to focus on tech, gadgets, and online-exclusive electronics deals.

Top Tech Categories for Cyber Monday:

- **Laptops and Computers**: Retailers like Dell, HP, and Lenovo often release special online-only deals.
- **Smart Home Devices**: Brands such as Amazon, Google, and Ring typically offer significant discounts on smart home products.
- **Software and Subscriptions**: Take advantage of promotions on software packages, streaming services, and digital subscriptions.

Tips for Tech Shopping:

- Check for online bundle deals that may not have been available during Black Friday.
- Review warranty and return policies specific to online purchases to avoid any surprises.

3. Explore Fashion and Apparel Sales

While Black Friday might focus more on electronics, Cyber Monday often highlights fashion, apparel, and beauty deals, with online retailers offering special discounts and free shipping.

What to Look For:

- **Apparel**: Check for markdowns on seasonal clothing, including winter wear and holiday outfits.
- **Beauty Products**: Online beauty retailers and department stores often have exclusive Cyber Monday sales on cosmetics and skincare.
- **Accessories**: Deals on bags, watches, and jewelry can often be found online post-Black Friday.

4. Extended Weekend Sales

Many retailers extend their Black Friday deals through the weekend, offering continuous promotions that lead into Cyber Monday.

Best Practices for Weekend Sales:

- **Monitor Websites**: Check retailer sites over the weekend for "early access" Cyber Monday deals.
- **Look for Bonus Offers**: Retailers may add additional perks such as gift cards, free gifts, or extra discounts for purchases over a certain amount.

Understanding the Importance of "Green Monday" and Other Late-Year Sales

While Black Friday and Cyber Monday dominate the headlines, other late-year sales events like "Green Monday" can offer surprising savings as the holiday season progresses.

1. What is Green Monday?

Green Monday, typically the second Monday in December, marks one of the last major shopping days before Christmas. Retailers often promote it as a final push for holiday sales, with competitive pricing and fast shipping options.

Why It's Important:

- **Last-Minute Deals**: It's one of the best opportunities for shoppers who need last-minute gifts or who missed out on Black Friday and Cyber Monday sales.
- **Holiday Shipping**: Green Monday promotions often include guarantees for delivery before Christmas, making it an attractive day for gift purchases.

Popular Green Monday Deals:

- **Electronics**: Retailers like Walmart and Best Buy often extend their tech discounts into Green Monday.
- **Toys and Gifts**: Expect to see deals on children's toys, games, and holiday gift sets.
- **Clothing and Accessories**: Seasonal markdowns continue as retailers clear out inventory for end-of-year accounting.

2. Other Late-Year Sales Events

Beyond Green Monday, keep an eye out for other sales events as the year comes to a close.

Examples of Late-Year Sales:

- **Free Shipping Day**: This one-day event, usually held in mid-December, promotes free shipping with guaranteed delivery by Christmas.
- **End-of-Year Clearance Sales**: As retailers look to clear out their inventory for new year stock, you can find deep discounts on a wide range of products.
- **Holiday Flash Sales**: Leading up to Christmas, some stores will offer surprise one-day or hourly sales to capture the attention of last-minute shoppers.

How to Prepare:

- **Create a Gift List**: Make a final list of gifts and essentials you still need, ensuring you don't miss these late-year opportunities.
- **Track Store Promotions**: Sign up for email alerts from your favorite retailers and follow them on social media for announcements of flash sales and special promotions.

Setting Reminders for Upcoming Price Drops

Keeping an eye on future price drops and potential promotions can help you snag additional deals even after Black Friday and Cyber Monday have passed.

1. Use Price Tracking Tools

Price tracking tools can monitor product prices over time and alert you when a significant drop occurs.

Top Price Tracking Tools:

- **Honey**: The Honey browser extension tracks price changes and applies discount codes automatically.
- **CamelCamelCamel**: This tool is specifically for tracking prices on Amazon and provides price history charts.
- **Keepa**: A robust tool for tracking Amazon price drops, including alerts for specific products.

How to Use These Tools:

- Enter the product link or name into the tracker.
- Set your desired price point or select the option for any price drop notification.
- Receive alerts via email or through the app when the price drops to your specified level.

2. Set Calendar Reminders for Key Dates

Using your digital calendar to set reminders for upcoming sales events helps you stay prepared.

Important Dates to Remember:

- **Green Monday**: Mark the second Monday of December for last-minute deals.

- **Free Shipping Day**: Add this event, typically mid-December, to your calendar as a reminder to finish holiday shopping with free shipping.
- **End-of-Year Sales**: Set reminders for post-Christmas clearance sales and New Year's deals.

Pro Tip: Create alerts for a few days before each event to give yourself time to browse deals and prepare a shopping list.

3. Sign Up for Retailer Newsletters

Retailers often send out exclusive discounts and early access deals to their email subscribers. Signing up for newsletters can keep you informed about upcoming promotions and surprise discounts.

Benefits of Newsletters:

- **Early Access**: Get early access to sales before they're made public.
- **Exclusive Coupons**: Receive coupon codes and special offers only available through the newsletter.
- **Personalized Recommendations**: Some retailers customize promotions based on your previous purchases or interests.

4. Watch for Price Adjustments

Many retailers offer a price adjustment policy where they'll refund you the difference if an item you bought goes on sale within a certain time frame after purchase.

How to Secure a Price Adjustment:

- **Check the Policy**: Familiarize yourself with the store's price adjustment window (usually between 7 and 14 days).
- **Keep Receipts**: Retain your purchase receipts or confirmation emails.
- **Act Quickly**: Contact the retailer as soon as you see the price drop to request the adjustment.

Final Thoughts

Following up on post-Black Friday deals involves strategic planning, awareness of key shopping events, and the use of price-tracking tools. By taking advantage of Cyber Monday, Green Monday, and other late-year sales, as well as setting reminders for upcoming price drops, you can make the most of the holiday shopping season. Staying informed and proactive will ensure that you find the best prices on gifts, essentials, and personal items well beyond the Black Friday rush.

Chapter 20: Reflecting and Preparing for Next Year

As Black Friday and the holiday shopping season come to a close, taking the time to reflect on your shopping successes and areas for improvement can provide valuable insights for the following year. Analyzing your experience helps fine-tune your strategies, ensuring that you maximize your savings and shopping efficiency in the future. This chapter will guide you through reviewing your shopping wins and losses, adjusting strategies based on this year's experience, and preparing early for next year's sales for a competitive edge.

Reviewing Your Shopping Wins and Losses

Evaluating your shopping performance from the past Black Friday and holiday sales season can help highlight what worked well and what needs improvement. By understanding your successes and challenges, you can develop a more effective strategy for next year.

1. Document Your Purchases and Savings

Start by creating a detailed record of the items you purchased, how much you spent, and the discounts you received.

Steps to Review Purchases:

- **Make a Comprehensive List**: Include the item, original price, sale price, percentage saved, and retailer.
- **Categorize Your Purchases**: Group your items by categories such as electronics, apparel, home goods, and gifts to see where you saved the most.
- **Calculate Total Savings**: Sum up your total expenditures and the savings to understand the overall financial impact.

Example Review Table:

Item	Original Price	Sale Price	% Saved	Retailer	Notes
4K TV	$900	$600	33%	Best Buy	Great door-buster deal
Winter Coat	$150	$90	40%	Macy's	Ran out of size quickly
Smart Speaker	$100	$50	50%	Amazon	Extra discount with promo code

2. Reflect on What Worked

Identify the strategies and tactics that yielded the best results. This could include using certain apps, timing purchases effectively, or shopping at specific retailers.

Questions to Ask:

- **Which purchases provided the most value?** Did you secure your high-priority items at great prices?
- **What strategies paid off?** Were there specific tools or approaches, such as price tracking apps or early access promotions, that worked particularly well?
- **Did you stay within your budget?** Evaluate how well you adhered to your pre-set spending plan.

3. Identify Areas for Improvement

Understanding where your shopping strategy fell short can help refine your approach for next year.

Common Challenges:

- **Missed Deals**: Note any high-priority items that you missed due to stock shortages or poor timing.
- **Impulse Buys**: Identify any purchases made on a whim that didn't add significant value.
- **Over-Extended Budget**: Assess where you may have spent more than intended and determine why.

Actionable Takeaways:

- Consider setting stricter guidelines for impulse purchases next year.
- Allocate more time to research items and retailers to avoid missed opportunities.
- Fine-tune your budget to ensure better adherence.

Adjusting Strategies Based on This Year's Experience

Based on your review, make adjustments to your shopping strategy to improve for next year's Black Friday and holiday sales. These changes can help streamline your shopping and make it more efficient.

1. Improve Your Budgeting Plan

If you found yourself overspending or underestimating costs, refine your budget for next year.

How to Adjust Your Budget:

- **Create Category Budgets**: Allocate spending limits for each category (e.g., electronics, clothing, gifts).
- **Set a Flexible Buffer**: Plan for a small buffer in your budget to account for unexpected but valuable purchases.
- **Track Expenses in Real Time**: Use a budget-tracking app to keep tabs on your spending as you shop.

2. Refine Your Deal-Finding Techniques

Evaluate which tools and apps were most effective and consider adding new resources for next year.

Improved Techniques:

- **Use Multiple Price Tracking Tools**: Don't rely solely on one price tracker; use several to cross-check prices.
- **Stay Updated on New Apps**: Keep an eye on emerging deal-finding tools that may be more effective or user-friendly.
- **Enhance Your Alerts**: Set more specific alerts for high-priority items to get instant notifications.

3. Plan Your Shopping Schedule Better

Timing is critical in securing the best deals, so analyze your shopping schedule and refine it for the future.

Adjustments to Consider:

- **Start Earlier**: If you found that early deals were better or sold out quickly, plan to shop earlier next year.
- **Plan for Downtime**: Schedule breaks to prevent fatigue, which can lead to poor decision-making and overspending.
- **Balance Online and In-Store Shopping**: If you struggled to balance both, plan your schedule to focus on the most promising method for each category.

4. Strengthen Your Tech Preparation

Ensure that your devices are optimized for a seamless shopping experience.

Tech Improvements:

- **Upgrade Devices**: If your device slowed down during peak shopping times, consider upgrading or optimizing it before next year.
- **Enhance Internet Connectivity**: Check your internet speed and consider temporary upgrades or using a hotspot for faster connections during high-traffic times.
- **Test Your Payment Methods**: Ensure your saved payment details are current and that your digital wallets and cards are up to date.

Starting Preparations Early for a Head Start on Future Sales

Early preparation can set you up for success and reduce the stress of last-minute decision-making.

1. Begin Researching Trends and Deals Early

Stay informed about product trends and predicted sales well before Black Friday.

Steps for Early Research:

- **Read Industry Reports**: Look for articles and reports that predict the best items to buy and anticipated discounts.
- **Monitor Retail Announcements**: Keep tabs on retailers' news to know when they release details about their Black Friday plans.
- **Create a Wishlist**: Compile a list of items you're considering purchasing and start tracking their prices months in advance to gauge true discounts.

2. Join Loyalty Programs and Memberships

Many retailers offer exclusive deals to members, so join loyalty programs early to receive perks like early access to sales.

Best Practices:

- **Join Reward Programs**: Sign up for loyalty programs at stores you plan to shop at well before Black Friday.
- **Check Membership Perks**: Review what benefits each loyalty program offers, such as early access, additional discounts, or free shipping.

3. Set Up Price Alerts in Advance

Set up price alerts for high-priority items months before Black Friday to get notifications as soon as prices drop.

How to Set Up Alerts:

- Use apps like Honey, CamelCamelCamel, and Keepa to track prices.
- Set specific price targets to be notified when an item drops below a certain cost.
- Adjust alerts as needed as Black Friday approaches and retailers announce promotions.

4. Prepare for Potential Challenges

Learn from past challenges and prepare solutions in advance to handle any obstacles.

Anticipated Challenges:

- **Website Crashes**: Be ready with multiple tabs open on different devices or know alternate retailers that carry the same product.
- **Stock Shortages**: Identify backup products or brands in case your top choice sells out.
- **Payment Issues**: Have a backup payment method ready, such as a secondary credit card or digital wallet, to avoid issues at checkout.

5. Stay Organized

Keeping all your shopping details organized helps streamline your efforts during the busy holiday season.

Organizational Tools:

- **Digital Planner**: Use a digital tool like Notion or Trello to keep track of wishlists, budgets, and purchase confirmations.
- **Receipt Management**: Create a folder in your email specifically for receipts and order confirmations to simplify returns and track spending.
- **Calendar Reminders**: Schedule reminders for major shopping events and last-minute sales like Cyber Monday and Green Monday.

Final Thoughts

Reflecting on your shopping experience and preparing for next year can greatly enhance your future success. By reviewing your wins and losses, adjusting your strategies, and starting your preparations early, you can set yourself up for a more organized, budget-friendly, and satisfying Black Friday shopping experience. This proactive approach ensures you're ready to tackle the holiday shopping season with confidence and efficiency, turning potential stress into an enjoyable and rewarding pursuit.

Appendix A: Black Friday Cheat Sheet

For a successful and streamlined Black Friday shopping experience, a quick reference guide is essential. This cheat sheet provides store opening times, the best apps and websites for finding deals, key phrases for effective negotiation, and a list of the top 10 items with the biggest markdowns. Use this appendix as your go-to guide for efficient shopping and smart decision-making.

Quick Reference for Store Opening Times, Best Apps, and Websites

1. Store Opening Times

Knowing when stores open can give you a competitive edge in securing high-demand items. Note that these times may vary by location, so check with your local store for precise hours.

Typical Store Opening Times for Black Friday:

- **Walmart**: Typically opens at 5:00 AM on Black Friday.
- **Best Buy**: Often opens at 5:00 AM; early access deals may start online.
- **Target**: Usually opens at 7:00 AM.
- **Macy's**: Opens around 6:00 AM, with online deals starting earlier.
- **Home Depot**: Generally opens at 6:00 AM.
- **Costco**: Opens at 9:00 AM; may offer exclusive member-only deals online.
- **Kohl's**: Typically opens at 5:00 AM.
- **JCPenney**: Often opens at 5:00 AM with doorbuster deals available.
- **GameStop**: Opens between 5:00-7:00 AM; check for specific store hours.

- **Amazon**: Online-only; deals start as early as midnight on Black Friday.

2. Best Apps and Websites for Deals

Using the right digital tools can streamline your shopping experience and help you stay on top of the best deals.

Top Apps for Black Friday Shopping:

- **Honey**: Automatically applies the best promo codes at checkout and tracks prices.
- **RetailMeNot**: Provides coupon codes and cashback offers for both online and in-store purchases.
- **Slickdeals**: Offers user-submitted and vetted deals, along with alerts for price drops.
- **Flipp**: Aggregates local flyers and ads to find the best deals in your area.
- **CamelCamelCamel**: Tracks Amazon price histories and alerts you to price drops.
- **ShopSavvy**: A barcode scanner that compares prices across online and local stores.
- **Rakuten**: Offers cashback on purchases when you shop through their platform.

Top Websites for Black Friday Deals:

- **BlackFriday.com**: Comprehensive listings of Black Friday ads and deals from major retailers.
- **DealNews**: Highlights curated lists of the best deals during Black Friday.
- **Amazon Black Friday**: Amazon's dedicated Black Friday section with deals that refresh throughout the day.
- **Best Buy Deals Page**: Best Buy's official deals page with featured promotions.

- **Target Weekly Ad**: Includes Black Friday deals and promotions.

Key Phrases for Effective Negotiation

Negotiating during Black Friday can be tricky, but using the right language can sometimes yield better results, especially for big-ticket items or in-store purchases. Here are key phrases that can help:

1. General Negotiation Phrases:

- *"Is this the best price you can offer?"*: A straightforward way to encourage the associate to look for additional discounts.
- *"I saw this item at [competitor] for [lower price]. Can you match or beat that?"*: Effective for price matching.
- *"Are there any additional discounts or promotions available today?"*: This opens the door for hidden discounts or manager approvals.
- *"If I buy more items or bundle this with another purchase, can I get a better deal?"*: Great for leveraging bulk purchases for discounts.

2. Phrases to Use with Customer Service:

- *"I'm a loyal customer and would love to continue shopping here. Is there anything more you can do on this price?"*: Subtly leverages your loyalty for potential discounts.
- *"I'd like to speak with a manager to see if there's any flexibility on this price."*: If the sales associate isn't authorized to negotiate, asking for a manager may help.
- *"I've seen similar deals with free shipping. Can you match that?"*: Useful for online purchases where shipping costs can add up.

3. Closing Negotiations:

- *"If you can include [e.g., free delivery, installation], I'm ready to make the purchase now."*: Adds value to your purchase without reducing the price.
- *"I'm comparing a few stores today, but I'd love to wrap this up here if the price can be adjusted slightly."*: Shows intent to buy while hinting at competition.

Top 10 Items with the Biggest Markdowns

Certain categories consistently offer the largest discounts during Black Friday. Here are the top 10 items that tend to see the biggest markdowns, based on historical data:

1. Televisions

- *Typical Markdowns*: 20-50% off
- *Best Brands*: LG, Samsung, Sony, TCL

2. Laptops

- *Typical Markdowns*: 15-40% off
- *Best Brands*: HP, Dell, Lenovo, MacBook models

3. Smart Home Devices

- *Typical Markdowns*: 30-60% off
- *Best Brands*: Amazon Echo, Google Nest, Ring doorbells

4. Gaming Consoles and Bundles

- *Typical Markdowns*: 10-25% off, often with included games or accessories
- *Top Consoles*: PlayStation, Xbox Series, Nintendo Switch

5. Home Appliances

- *Typical Markdowns*: 20-40% off
- *Best Brands*: Whirlpool, GE, Samsung, KitchenAid

6. Headphones and Earbuds

- *Typical Markdowns*: 25-50% off
- *Best Brands*: Bose, Sony, Apple AirPods, JBL

7. Clothing and Apparel

- *Typical Markdowns*: 30-70% off
- *Best Categories*: Winter coats, jeans, athleisure, and accessories

8. Kitchenware

- *Typical Markdowns*: 20-60% off
- *Best Brands*: Instant Pot, Ninja, Cuisinart, Le Creuset

9. Toys and Games

- *Typical Markdowns*: 20-50% off
- *Top Picks*: LEGO sets, board games, branded action figures

10. Beauty and Personal Care Products

- *Typical Markdowns*: 20-50% off
- *Top Brands*: Dyson (hair tools), Sephora exclusive sets, skincare brands like Olay and Neutrogena

Final Thoughts

This Black Friday Cheat Sheet is designed to give you quick, easy access to the most important information for a successful shopping experience. Use it to plan your day, negotiate effectively, and target the items with the biggest markdowns. With the right tools and strategies, you'll be prepared to make smart purchases and secure the best deals.

Appendix B: Budgeting Worksheets and Shopping List Templates

Planning your Black Friday shopping with organized worksheets and templates can greatly enhance your ability to stay on budget and track your expenses efficiently. This appendix provides a comprehensive guide to printable budget planners, customizable shopping list formats, and expense trackers to help you manage your shopping before, during, and after Black Friday. These tools are designed to streamline your process and ensure you make the most out of your shopping experience.

Printable Budget Planners

A budget planner is an essential tool for setting spending limits and allocating your resources effectively across different categories. Below are detailed templates you can use to organize your finances.

1. Total Budget Overview Worksheet

This worksheet helps you allocate your overall Black Friday budget into different categories such as electronics, clothing, gifts, and home goods.

Template Details:

- **Total Budget**: Enter your total planned spending amount for Black Friday.
- **Category Breakdown**: List categories and allocate a budget for each.
- **Percentage Allocation**: Indicate what percentage of your total budget is dedicated to each category for a balanced approach.

Example:

Category	Budget Allocated	Percentage of Total Budget
Electronics	$500	30%
Clothing	$300	18%

Category	Budget Allocated	Percentage of Total Budget
Gifts	$400	24%
Home Goods	$250	15%
Miscellaneous	$150	9%
Total	**$1,600**	**100%**

2. Detailed Category Budget Worksheet

For more detailed planning, use category-specific worksheets that break down the budget within each section. This template helps you list items, their expected prices, and your budget cap for that category.

Template Details:

- **Item Name**: Specific product or gift.
- **Expected Cost**: Estimated or advertised price.
- **Max Budget**: Your spending limit for that item.
- **Notes**: Additional information such as store names or online sites.

Example:

Item	Expected Cost	Max Budget	Notes
4K TV	$450	$500	Best Buy, early access
Winter Coat	$75	$90	Macy's
Smart Speaker	$50	$60	Amazon, Cyber Monday deal

Customizable Shopping List Formats

Keeping track of items you plan to purchase helps ensure you don't miss any essential buys and prevents impulse purchases. Use the following templates to organize your shopping list.

1. Basic Shopping List Template

A simple template that includes essential details for quick reference while shopping.

Template Details:

- **Item**: Product name.
- **Store/Website**: Where you plan to purchase the item.
- **Price**: Expected price or range.
- **Priority**: Label items as high, medium, or low priority to focus on must-haves first.

Example:

Item	Store/Website	Price	Priority
Noise-Cancelling Headphones	Best Buy	$200	High
Instant Pot	Walmart	$70	Medium
Kids' LEGO Set	Target	$40	Low

2. Advanced Shopping List with Timelines

This template helps organize items based on when they go on sale, ensuring you're prepared for flash sales and timed promotions.

Template Details:

- **Item**: Name of the product.
- **Store/Website**: Place to purchase.
- **Sale Time**: When the sale starts (include time zones).
- **Price**: Sale price.
- **Notes**: Any additional sale details (e.g., promo codes or doorbuster notes).

Example:

Item	Store/Website	Sale Time	Price	Notes
Gaming Laptop	Newegg	Midnight EST	$800	Promo code required
Designer Handbag	Nordstrom	6:00 AM PST	$120	Limited stock, early bird
Robot Vacuum	Amazon	12:00 AM PST	$250	Part of "lightning deal"

Expense Trackers for Post-Black Friday Analysis

Tracking your spending after Black Friday helps you evaluate how well you stayed within your budget and highlights areas for improvement. These expense trackers are designed to make post-event analysis easy and effective.

1. Purchase Log for Expense Tracking

Log all your Black Friday purchases to track spending in real-time and review after the event.

Template Details:

- **Date**: Date of purchase.
- **Item**: Product name.
- **Store/Website**: Where you bought it.
- **Actual Cost**: Amount spent.
- **Budgeted Cost**: Initial budget for comparison.
- **Difference**: Indicate if you stayed within, exceeded, or saved money on each item.

Example:

Date	Item	Store/Website	Actual Cost	Budgeted Cost	Difference
11/24	4K TV	Best Buy	$450	$500	-$50
11/24	Smart Speaker	Amazon	$45	$60	-$15
11/24	Winter Coat	Macy's	$95	$90	+$5

2. Expense Analysis Worksheet

This tool helps you evaluate your overall spending after Black Friday, identifying which categories stayed within budget and which exceeded it.

Template Details:

- **Category**: The type of product (e.g., electronics, clothing).
- **Total Spent**: Sum of all purchases in that category.
- **Budgeted Amount**: Initial budget for the category.
- **Difference**: Positive or negative difference indicating how well you adhered to your budget.

Example:

Category	Total Spent	Budgeted Amount	Difference	Notes
Electronics	$480	$500	-$20	Stayed under budget
Clothing	$310	$300	+$10	Slightly over, adjust next year
Gifts	$390	$400	-$10	Well managed

How to Use These Worksheets and Templates

1. **Print or Save Digitally**: Print the worksheets for manual entry or save them as editable PDFs for use on your computer or tablet.
2. **Pre-Fill Basic Details**: Enter known information, such as anticipated prices or sales times, before Black Friday.
3. **Update in Real-Time**: Track purchases and spending during Black Friday to monitor your budget.
4. **Review and Reflect**: Post-Black Friday, review your completed expense trackers and worksheets to analyze your shopping behavior and identify improvements for next year.

Final Thoughts

Appendix B equips you with the tools to plan, manage, and analyze your Black Friday shopping effectively. From budgeting planners and shopping list templates to post-event expense trackers, these resources ensure that your shopping is organized, budget-conscious, and successful. By using these worksheets and templates, you can approach Black Friday with confidence and prepare for a smoother, more strategic experience year after year.

Appendix C: Cybersecurity and Online Safety Checklist

Ensuring cybersecurity and practicing safe online shopping are essential, especially during Black Friday and holiday sales when cyber threats are more prevalent. This appendix provides a comprehensive checklist to set up secure browsing, manage passwords effectively, and avoid common scams such as phishing and identity theft. Use these guidelines to protect your data and shop with confidence.

Step-by-Step Guide for Setting Up Secure Browsing

Safe browsing habits and secure connections are critical when shopping online. Follow these steps to protect your personal and financial information.

1. Use a Secure Internet Connection

Shopping over public Wi-Fi can expose your data to hackers. Always use a secure, private network.

Steps to Ensure a Secure Connection:

- **Shop from Home**: Whenever possible, use your secured home Wi-Fi network.
- **Use a VPN**: A Virtual Private Network (VPN) encrypts your internet connection, hiding your IP address and keeping your data safe from prying eyes.
  - *Top VPNs*: NordVPN, ExpressVPN, CyberGhost
- **Turn Off Auto-Connect to Wi-Fi**: Ensure your device doesn't automatically connect to unsecured networks.

2. Update Your Browser and Security Software

Ensure your browser and any security software are up-to-date to protect against the latest threats.

Checklist for Browser and Software Updates:

- **Browser Version**: Verify that your web browser is running the latest version.
- **Security Software**: Update your antivirus and anti-malware programs.
- **Install Security Add-Ons**: Add extensions such as HTTPS Everywhere and uBlock Origin to your browser for extra protection.

3. Enable Multi-Factor Authentication (MFA)

Adding an extra layer of security through MFA can prevent unauthorized access even if your password is compromised.

How to Set Up MFA:

- **Enable on Shopping Sites**: Log into your accounts (e.g., Amazon, eBay) and go to the security settings to enable MFA.
- **Choose Verification Methods**: Use an authenticator app (e.g., Google Authenticator, Authy) or SMS codes.
- **Backup Codes**: Save backup codes in a secure location for emergency access.

Password Management Tips and Tools

Strong, unique passwords for each account are essential for online safety. Follow these guidelines for effective password management.

1. Create Strong Passwords

A good password should be long, unique, and difficult for others to guess.

Characteristics of a Strong Password:

- **Length**: At least 12-16 characters.
- **Complexity**: Use a mix of uppercase and lowercase letters, numbers, and special characters.
- **Avoid Personal Information**: Don't use easily guessed data like names, birthdates, or common words.

2. Use a Password Manager

Password managers help generate and store complex passwords securely, so you don't have to remember them all.

Recommended Password Managers:

- **LastPass**: Offers secure storage, password generation, and cross-device syncing.
- **1Password**: Includes advanced security features like password auditing.
- **Bitwarden**: An open-source and budget-friendly option with strong encryption.

How to Use a Password Manager:

- **Install the App**: Download and install the password manager on your devices.

- **Create a Strong Master Password**: This is the only password you need to remember.
- **Store Credentials**: Save login information for shopping sites, payment platforms, and email accounts.

3. Change Passwords Periodically

Updating your passwords regularly reduces the risk of long-term account compromise.

Best Practices for Password Updates:

- **Change Every 3-6 Months**: Rotate passwords to ensure ongoing protection.
- **Set Reminders**: Schedule reminders on your calendar for password updates.
- **Avoid Reusing Old Passwords**: Always create fresh, unique passwords for each update.

Best Practices for Avoiding Phishing and Identity Theft

Phishing scams and identity theft are significant risks during busy shopping periods. Implement these practices to avoid falling victim to scams.

1. Recognize Phishing Emails and Messages

Phishing emails are designed to look like legitimate communications but contain malicious links or attachments.

How to Spot a Phishing Email:

- **Sender Address**: Verify the sender's email address. Legitimate businesses will use a consistent domain (e.g., @store.com, not @store-offers.info).
- **Urgency and Pressure**: Be cautious of messages that demand immediate action or threaten account suspension.
- **Generic Greetings**: Emails addressed as "Dear Customer" or "Valued User" instead of your name can be a red flag.
- **Suspicious Links**: Hover over any links to see the URL destination without clicking.

2. Avoid Clicking Unverified Links

Links in emails and social media posts can lead to phishing sites designed to steal your information.

Safety Tips for Handling Links:

- **Verify Links**: Always type the URL into your browser instead of clicking on a link from an email or text.
- **Check the URL Carefully**: Ensure it starts with "https" and the domain name matches the official website.
- **Use a Link Scanner**: Online tools like VirusTotal can help check if a link is safe before you visit it.

3. Protect Personal Information

Be mindful of what personal information you share online, especially during the checkout process.

Steps to Limit Personal Data Sharing:

- **Use Minimal Data**: Only provide the information necessary to complete your purchase.
- **Avoid Public Sharing**: Don't post personal details such as your address or phone number in public forums or on social media.
- **Use Alias Emails**: Create an alias email specifically for shopping to separate it from your main account and reduce exposure to spam.

4. Monitor Your Financial Accounts

Keep an eye on your bank and credit card accounts for unauthorized transactions, especially during the holiday shopping season.

How to Monitor Your Accounts:

- **Set Up Alerts**: Enable transaction notifications to receive real-time updates for purchases.
- **Review Statements**: Check your account statements regularly for any suspicious or unexpected charges.
- **Report Issues Quickly**: If you spot any fraudulent activity, contact your bank or credit card company immediately to secure your accounts and request a replacement card if needed.

5. Be Cautious with Public Wi-Fi

Using public Wi-Fi can expose your data to hackers who intercept connections to steal sensitive information.

Tips for Safe Public Wi-Fi Use:

- **Avoid Shopping on Public Wi-Fi**: If possible, use a mobile data connection or wait until you're on a secure network.

- **Use a VPN**: A VPN encrypts your data and keeps your activity private, even on public Wi-Fi.
- **Disable File Sharing**: Ensure that file sharing and other vulnerable services are turned off when connected to public Wi-Fi.

Cybersecurity Checklist for Black Friday Shopping

Use this quick checklist to ensure you're prepared for safe online shopping:

1. **Update all devices and software to the latest versions.**
2. **Use a VPN when connecting to public or unsecured Wi-Fi.**
3. **Enable multi-factor authentication (MFA) on your accounts.**
4. **Use a password manager for strong, unique passwords.**
5. **Verify the legitimacy of websites and links before clicking.**
6. **Monitor your financial accounts for unauthorized transactions.**
7. **Set transaction alerts for real-time notifications.**
8. **Be cautious of emails or messages urging immediate action.**
9. **Shop only on sites with "https" in the URL.**
10. **Never save payment information on unfamiliar or non-secure sites.**

Final Thoughts

Cybersecurity is an essential part of any online shopping strategy, especially during high-traffic events like Black Friday. By following the steps in this guide, using password management tools, and staying vigilant against phishing and identity theft, you can protect your personal and financial information while shopping confidently.

<u>Message from the Author:</u>

I hope you enjoyed this book, I love astrology and knew there was not a book such as this out on the shelf. I love metaphysical items as well. Please check out my other books:

-Life of Government Benefits

-My life of Hell

-My life with Hydrocephalus

-Red Sky

-World Domination:Woman's rule

-World Domination:Woman's Rule 2: The War

-Life and Banishment of Apophis: book 1

-The Kidney Friendly Diet

-The Ultimate Hemp Cookbook

-Creating a Dispensary(legally)

-Cleanliness throughout life: the importance of showering from childhood to adulthood.

-Strong Roots: The Risks of Overcoddling children

-Hemp Horoscopes: Cosmic Insights and Earthly Healing

- Celestial Hemp Navigating the Zodiac: Through the Green Cosmos

-Astrological Hemp: Aligning The Stars with Earth's Ancient Herb

-The Astrological Guide to Hemp: Stars, Signs, and Sacred Leaves

-Green Growth: Innovative Marketing Strategies for your Hemp Products and Dispensary

-Cosmic Cannabis

-Astrological Munchies

-Henry The Hemp

-Zodiacal Roots: The Astrological Soul Of Hemp

- **Green Constellations: Intersection of Hemp and Zodiac**

-Hemp in The Houses: An astrological Adventure Through The Cannabis Galaxy

-Galactic Ganja Guide

Heavenly Hemp
Zodiac Leaves
Doctor Who Astrology
Cannastrology
Stellar Satvias and Cosmic Indicas
Celestial Cannabis: A Zodiac Journey
AstroHerbology: The Sky and The Soil: Volume 1
AstroHerbology:Celestial Cannabis:Volume 2
Cosmic Cannabis Cultivation
The Starry Guide to Herbal Harmony: Volume 1
The Starry Guide to Herbal Harmony: Cannabis Universe: Volume 2

Yugioh Astrology: Astrological Guide to Deck, Duels and more
Nightmarc Mansion: Echoes of The Abyss
Nightmare Mansion 2: Legacy of Shadows
Nightmare Mansion 3: Shadows of the Forgotten
Nightmare Mansion 4: Echoes of the Damned
The Life and Banishment of Apophis: Book 2
Nightmare Mansion: Halls of Despair
Healing with Herb: Cannabis and Hydrocephalus
Planetary Pot: Aligning with Astrological Herbs: Volume 1
Fast Track to Freedom: 30 Days to Financial Independence Using AI, Assets, and Agile Hustles
Cosmic Hemp Pathways
How to Become Financially Free in 30 Days: 10,000 Paths to Prosperity
Zodiacal Herbage: Astrological Insights: Volume 1
Nightmare Mansion: Whispers in the Walls
The Daleks Invade Atlantis
Henry the hemp and Hydrocephalus

10X The Kidney Friendly Diet
Cannabis Universe: Adult coloring book

Hemp Astrology: The Healing Power of the Stars

Zodiacal Herbage: Astrological Insights: Cannabis Universe: Volume 2

<u>**Planetary Pot: Aligning with Astrological Herbs: Cannabis Universes: Volume 2**</u>

Doctor Who Meets the Replicators and SG-1: The Ultimate Battle for Survival

Nightmare Mansion: Curse of the Blood Moon

<u>**The Celestial Stoner: A Guide to the Zodiac**</u>

Cosmic Pleasures: Sex Toy Astrology for Every Sign

Hydrocephalus Astrology: Navigating the Stars and Healing Waters

Lapis and the Mischievous Chocolate Bar

Celestial Positions: Sexual Astrology for Every Sign

Apophis's Shadow Work Journal: **:** A Journey of Self-Discovery and Healing

Kinky Cosmos: Sexual Kink Astrology for Every Sign

Digital Cosmos: The Astrological Digimon Compendium

Stellar Seeds: The Cosmic Guide to Growing with Astrology

Apophis's Daily Gratitude Journal

Cat Astrology: Feline Mysteries of the Cosmos

The Cosmic Kama Sutra: An Astrological Guide to Sexual Positions

Unleash Your Potential: A Guided Journal Powered by AI Insights

Whispers of the Enchanted Grove

Cosmic Pleasures: An Astrological Guide to Sexual Kinks

369, 12 Manifestation Journal

Whisper of the nocturne journal(blank journal for writing or drawing)

The Boogey Book

Locked In Reflection: A Chastity Journey Through Locktober

Generating Wealth Quickly:

How to Generate $100,000 in 24 Hours

Star Magic: Harness the Power of the Universe

The Flatulence Chronicles: A Fart Journal for Self-Discovery

The Doctor and The Death Moth

Seize the Day: A Personal Seizure Tracking Journal

The Ultimate Boogeyman Safari: A Journey into the Boogie World and Beyond

Whispers of Samhain: 1,000 Spells of Love, Luck, and Lunar Magic: Samhain Spell Book

Apophis's guides:

Witch's Spellbook Crafting Guide for Halloween

<u>Frost & Flame: The Enchanted Yule Grimoire of 1000 Winter Spells</u>

<u>The Ultimate Boogey Goo Guide & Spooky Activities for Halloween Fun</u>

Harmony of the Scales: A Libra's Spellcraft for Balance and Beauty

The Enchanted Advent: 36 Days of Christmas Wonders

Nightmare Mansion: The Labyrinth of Screams

Harvest of Enchantment: 1,000 Spells of Gratitude, Love, and Fortune for Thanksgiving

The Boogey Chronicles: A Journal of Nightly Encounters and Shadowy Secrets

The 12 Days of Financial Freedom: A Step-by-Step Christmas Countdown to Transform Your Finances

Sigil of the Eternal Spiral Blank Journal

A Christmas Feast: Timeless Recipes for Every Meal

Holiday Stress-Free Solutions: A Survival Guide to Thriving During the Festive Season

Yu-Gi-Oh! Holiday Gifting Mastery: The Ultimate Guide for Fans and Newcomers Alike

Holiday Harmony: A Hydrocephalus Survival Guide for the Festive Season

Celestial Craft: The Witch's Almanac for 2025 – A Cosmic Guide to Manifestations, Moons, and Mystical Events

Doctor Who: The Toymaker's Winter Wonderland

Tulsa King Unveiled: A Thrilling Guide to Stallone's Mafia Masterpiece

Pendulum Craft: A Complete Guide to Crafting and Using Personalized Divination Tools

Nightmare Mansion: Santa's Eternal Eve

Starlight Noel: A Cosmic Journey through Christmas Mysteries

The Dark Architect: Unlocking the Blueprint of Existence

Surviving the Embrace: The Ultimate Guide to Encounters with The Hugging Molly

The Enchanted Codex: Secrets of the Craft for Witches, Wiccans, and Pagans

Harvest of Gratitude: A Complete Thanksgiving Guide

Yuletide Essentials: A Complete Guide to an Authentic and Magical Christmas

Celestial Smokes: A Cosmic Guide to Cigars and Astrology

Living in Balance: A Comprehensive Survival Guide to Thriving with Diabetes Insipidus

Cosmic Symbiosis: The Venom Zodiac Chronicles

The Cursed Paw of Ambition

Cosmic Symbiosis: The Astrological Venom Journal

Celestial Wonders Unfold: A Stargazer's Guide to the Cosmos (2024-2029)

If you want solar for your home go here: https://www.harborso-lar.live/apophisenterprises/

Get Some Tarot cards: https://www.makeplayingcards.com/sell/
apophis-occult-shop

Get some shirts: https://www.bonfire.com/store/apophis-shirt-emporium/

Instagrams:
@apophis_enterprises,
@apophisbookemporium,
@apophisscardshop
Twitter: @apophisenterpr1
Tiktok:@apophisenterprise
Youtube: @sg1fan23477, @FiresideRetreatKingdom
Hive: @sg1fan23477
CheeLee: @SG1fan23477

Podcast: Apophis Chat Zone: https://open.spotify.com/show/5zXbrCLEV2xzCp8ybrfHsk?si=fb4d4fdbdce44dec

Newsletter: https://apophiss-newsletter-27c897.beehiiv.com/